Golf in the Wild

Golf in the Wild

A journey through time and place

Robin J. Down

First published in the United Kingdom in 2014 by

northumbrian : light

ISBN 978-0-9928717-0-3

Contents

Acknowledgements

In no particular order except the first, my wife and my rock, Pam, who, together with her Dad, Ramsey, made everything possible. As a non-golfer, her dedication to the task of research and 'caddying' was throughout, above and beyond the call of duty. Pam was also an editor. This sterling effort was supported by my good friend Norman Harris and someone who has chosen to remain anonymous but whose contribution is still appreciated. This combined effort did much to improve the original manuscript. I am forever indebted.

I would never have thought to write this book without first reading Andrew Greig's wonderful *Preferred Lies*. He demonstrates, in pitch perfect prose, how writing about golf is much enhanced by digression. Then there are the Geordie Daves who are mentioned in the Introduction to this book – they got me started on this obsessional pastime. Messrs Atkinson, Humble and Turnbull, I blame you entirely for this (and much more besides). There is a fourth Dave from the Scottish Borders who is absolved from all guilt.

To the members of Allendale Golf Club, past and present, thank you for your company, friendship and the many happy rounds of golf across a piece of land which I have come to know intimately – especially the deep rough. Along with the golf there has been many a happy BBQ, quiz night, fancy dress evening and even, but only once, karaoke. My rendition of *Urban Spaceman* was so 'memorable' that the event has never been repeated. In particular I would like to single out Ian and Michael (the greenkeepers). Mike (the glider), Colin and Fran, Ian (the L plate), John and Alwyn, Ian and Valeria and the Honourable Member for Bury.

If there is one chapter of which I am particularly fond, it is Killin. I am indebted to Gillean Ford who was not only a source for invaluable historical information but was kind enough to offer significant help and advice to a complete stranger.

Similarly, the chapter on Selkirk is much enhanced by the inclusion of pictures and information relating to the Robert D. Clapperton Daylight Photographic Studio. I am grateful to Jane Mitchell and Aileen Wilson of the Robert D. Clapperton Trust who granted the necessary permissions and were kind enough to enable access to their fascinating museum. In researching this book, my primary intention was to arrive and play each course as a casual visitor; however, inevitably, when I put the metaphorical pen to paper, questions arose. All of the courses detailed in this book are small and for the most part run by volunteers who already give freely of their time. I am therefore indebted to all of those who gave yet more in answering my phone calls and questions. In particular I would like to offer special thanks to Sylvia Milburn at Allendale, Ian Davison at Bishopshire, Jack Shaw-Stewart at Traigh and John Macleod at Ullapool.

All of the images in this book are from my own collection except where stated. I am grateful to the Department of Special Collections, University of St Andrews Library for providing a series of Valentine postcard images and advising on their reproduction. Similarly, I am grateful to Allendale Golf Club for use of their centenary images; The Mitchell Library, Glasgow City Council for granting permission to reproduce the picture of Killin Station from the G. H. Robin Collection; Killin Golf Club for reproduction of their historical photographs; Craignure Golf Club for reproduction of the 1980 fly-past commemorating the club's reopening.

Finally I must make it clear that the only real art in this book is the drawings at the start of each chapter. These were created by my youngest son, James (www.gingerbrown.org.uk), the real artistic talent in the family. The book would be much the poorer without them.

Introduction

This book has been a long time in the making. I was introduced to the game late in life by three Geordies, by coincidence, all of them called Dave. They either saved or condemned me, depending on your point of view. They are a beguiling tribe and, once you get tuned into the dialect, well-meaning and friendly. I was so taken by them that I married one – a Geordie, not a Dave. It was Easter Monday 2000 when I was first let loose on a course in the company of one of the said Daves and I have hardly stopped hitting golf balls since. It has preserved my sanity or sent me quite mad, again depending on your point of view.

An example of my madness is that, quite early in my 'career', I volunteered to become *Honorary Treasurer* at Allendale Golf Club, deep in the high hills of Northumberland, a post I have held for more than ten years. This has given me an insight into the trials and tribulations of running a small club based almost entirely on volunteers. Consequently, I declare my financial interest from the outset. This book is intended to encourage golfers to visit these very special courses in out-of-the-way places which are dependent on the continuing support of the casual visitor. Green fees are an important aspect of the bottom line. Take up the challenge to play all of the courses described and you will not only appreciate their delights but also why they must continue to exist. The sport would be much the poorer without them.

Golf in the Wild is no ordinary golf book, some might say it is hardly a golf book at all. There are certainly long passages when the game is hardly mentioned, instead it heads off in a wide divergent arc through history, ghosts and the passing of time. In short, much of it is simply about life and so is our obsession with this pointless pastime. We play the game as we play life and we cannot help ourselves. You will find no golfing tips in this book. I am only qualified to advise on one medical aspect of the game – if there is an honesty box, *always* cough up!

The digressions are also intended as light relief for the author and the reader. Golf is simply not a subject that you can write about with unending flair and interest. At its most fundamental level it can be summarised as *man hits ball, walks and then hits ball again* – there is not even an opponent attempting a sliding tackle, nor an in-fielder hovering in the slips to catch that unintended nick off the bat. In many ways what makes golf interesting to the happy hacking amateur are the many and varied places in which the game can be played and this is primarily the purpose of *Golf in the Wild* – to explore the possibilities for playing this most frustrating of games in wild, beautiful and unexpected places.

The journey starts at the centre of mainland Britain and heads, via a circuitous route, to its top left-hand corner. I have chosen this route to the far reaches of Scotland's north west coast because it is the most spectacular of any in Britain and, I would suggest, anywhere in the world – to appreciate this there is no substitute for going there yourself.

The golf courses visited are, to some extent, determined by the route, but they have certain attributes in common: they are all 9 holes, they are generally quiet with honesty boxes and they are all in beautiful settings – in short, they are just like Allendale, the starting point for this journey into the wild. I hesitate to describe this book as a guide, although at its heart that is the intention and consequently there is a loosely described route which does its utmost to avoid motorways and urban conurbations; *Golf in the Wild* is as much about the journey as the golf courses discovered along the way. Consequently, the route also digresses and makes no attempt at the shortest possible time between destinations – the assumption is that the reader enjoys the drive behind the wheel as much as the drive from the tee.

The reference to 'we' throughout is by no means Royal, my life and this journey have never been a solitary endeavour. 'We' relates to three different people all of whom were once very special – my wife, Pam, remains so.

The journey also allows me a diversion down the slipstream of motor racing history, an obsession from my youth. This sport shaped me, distracted me at school when I should have been paying more attention, and in many ways determined my fate, which in turn influenced what I became and therefore how I play golf. The racing history starts in the early 1960s and finishes on a fateful date in 1973, a timespan which coincides with my teenage obsession. The recent upsurge in interest with these years, as depicted in the films *Rush* and *1:Life on the Limit*, is coincidental but hardly surprising. Anyone who witnessed motor racing in those years, however much from the sidelines, was inevitably marked by a seemingly endless series of tragic events.

Other great influences on my golf swing have been family and relationships, all of which appear regularly in this book; everything is interconnected. I was the absolute opposite of a 'mummy's boy' but my mother and her parents, aunts and uncles do feature large among these pages. This is because we were at war from my earliest teenage years, from the time I tried to exert a serious will of my own. Throughout the book she is variously referred to as Peg, Peggy, Mother or Mum dependent on the circumstances I am describing and the way I feel about the associated events. I had considered editing in some consistency but thought better of it – Peg was so many different people that no single name fits; in the end, confined to a care home, she became known as Marian, just to emphasise my point.

It is perhaps unfair to expose her in print; I am sure my sons could relate worse about me, but this is my story, my version of the truth. Peg's version would be different, but she never chose to write it down, indeed, she would have thoroughly disapproved of the whole endeavour. The only literary character I can find who resembles Peg is Constance Winterson, the tyrant known as 'my Mother' in Jeanette Winterson's *Oranges Are Not The Only Fruit.*

Of an almost identical age, they were both the product of a Victorian upbringing which had unintended consequences for the children they raised. Unlike Constance, Peg was no missionary, indeed she was fundamentally atheistic, but would never have admitted as much in polite company. However, there were similarities in their approaches to discipline, bordering on the abusive, and their pronouncements, tinged with madness. The other common ground is that they were, for the most part, well-intentioned and only wanted to provide protection from the dangerous world outside. They were doomed to fail.

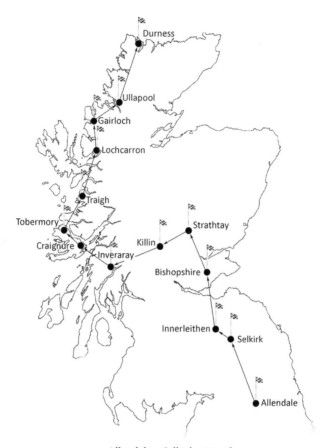

Allendale – Selkirk: 77 miles

Selkirk – Innerleithen: 15 miles

Innerleithen – Bishopshire: 74 miles

Bishopshire – Strathtay: 48 miles

Strathtay – Killin: 28 miles

Killin – Rest and Be Thankful – Inveraray: 54 miles

Inveraray – Oban – Craignure (ferry) – Tobermory: 70 miles

Tobermory – Kilchoan (ferry) – Sanna – Traigh: 66 miles

Traigh – Mallaig – Armadale (ferry) – Ord – Plockton – Lochcarron: 68 miles

Lochcarron – Applecross – Gairloch: 79 miles

Gairloch – Ullapool: 56 miles

Ullapool – Inverpolly – Sandwood Bay – Durness: 92 miles

Approximately 727 inspiring miles

1 Allendale

Everyone agreed it would be a
miracle indeed if the boy survived
Paul Simon – *Bookends* [1]

In the far corner of Allendale village square there is a handsome lychgate which leads to St Cuthbert's Church. On the south aisle wall near the tower hangs a sundial inscribed with *latitude 54° 50'* in support of the nineteenth Century claim that Allendale is at the very centre of Britain. The methods for establishing this centre point are many and varied, leading to widely differing claims and counter-claims. It is an inconvenient truth that, even using the 'St Cuthbert method', the centre is now more accurately positioned some nine miles to the north west, in the town of Haltwhistle, an assertion enthusiastically supported by the town's Centre of Britain Hotel. I will ignore this; for the purposes of this journey I am starting at the centre of Britain and heading for its top left corner, Cape Wrath. To paraphrase Joy Division's bass player, Peter Hook, *'This book is the truth, the whole truth and nothing but the truth ... excepting the preferred lies' – Unknown Pleasures, Inside Joy Division.*

Allendale Golf Club is almost a spiritual home; set high in the Allen Valley it is a spectacular place to play the game, it is the course I know best and as a first-rate hacker, I have visited most of its far-flung corners. I came to the sport late in life and like many of my contemporaries regret the years lost to other less-rewarding pursuits; getting married (twice), having children (three) and consuming alcohol (too much). Firm in the belief that my game would be so much improved had I but started as a boy, in reality I stood no chance – golf was never mentioned at home. My Dad was a conventional sportsman and of his time. Raised in Hampshire, he was Andover Grammar School football and cricket captain in 1939 and went on to play both for his university. A quiet man, he would not have enjoyed nor endured the gin-soaked opinions of austere Tory clubhouses – like father, like son. It was only very late in life that the possibility of golf was ever mentioned, enthused by a neighbour when in his seventies. Naturally reserved, diminished by age and subject to an eternally bossy wife, the idea was soon discarded – *'You don't want to do that Ken, think of your back'*. Sport in general is a window on the man and his character, and golf in particular is a wide open door. Nothing exposes the inner mind more than self-inflicted hardship. I was only ever exposed to his sporting character on a tennis court where he was always fair but fiercely competitive. It is a pity that we never stood together on a tee box; no first, nor final rounds.

In truth, if I had started very young I may briefly have seen a single-figure handicap, but so much of golf is played in the head and that part of my anatomy is not best suited to the game and never has been;

I would be a supreme test for a sports psychologist. Standing over a ball with the driver in hand, my 'swing thoughts' can be positive, less positive with irons and 'positively negative' with a putter in hand. On so many occasions I firmly believe a putt will not drop and on so many occasions I prove myself right – *'there, you see, I told you so'* – the power of self-fulfilling prophecies. No, the truth is I am a bogey golfer, happy to play off 18 and resentful when a par does not yield 3 stableford points. There are occasional days when the golfing gods look down with some benevolence and the putts tumble in, or more likely, the chips cosy up to the hole and the next stroke is taken with a happy certainty. It is for days like this we keep turning out, deluded into believing that this is our real game and the rest an aberration.

Consequently, I seek out places where a middling golfer can enjoy his game, unintimidated by the course, crowded fairways or over-sized saloons with over-sized owners wallowing in over-sized car parks. I want to be relaxed by golf, I want visual stimulus and I want to be elevated by the experience, not depressed. Allendale does all of these things and much more, thus providing the template for the courses that make up the pilgrimage described in the rest of this book. Most of all, the chosen courses have their own character based entirely on the natural contours of the land and have not been carved out of the landscape with a fleet of excavators; they stand alone and defiant as *'the noose of uniformity winds ever tighter around the planet'*.[2]

The Allendale course is tucked away in the hills of an Area of Out-standing Natural Beauty and must therefore be discreet. The road south out of Allendale winds up the Allen Valley along the B6295 towards Allenheads, following the course of the East Allen River. A mile or so south of the town, as the road breaks free from overhanging trees, a sharp left turn is signposted to the club. The track is rutted, rabbits run for cover and, depending on the time of year, it will wear a layer of rich agricultural muck. This unpretentious approach climbs

167 feet in a third of a mile, which is more or less the difference between the high and low ground on the course; it helps to be fit. The clubhouse sits at 1,077 feet above sea level on the west-facing side of Green Hill which peaks at 1,374 feet – it is not a complete exaggeration to suggest the course is situated on the side of a mountain. A wind turbine installed in 2010 marks your arrival; it powers the clubhouse and generates much-needed additional income from excess electricity feeding into the National Grid. On a plain 9-metre tower with dark-coloured blades, it blends into the agricultural landscape in a manner reminiscent of the iconic multi-bladed windpumps of America's central plains.

The club's official address is High Studdon, which is actually the farm further up the hill. The postcode has been specifically allocated to mislead those relying on satellite navigation; much better to get out the Ordnance Survey map[3] and look for the small blue flag. You will see that the greens and fairways are surrounded by The Hagg, The Spittal, Stob Cross, Scotch Halls, Herds Law and Haggburn Gate – strange names with history.

Fittingly, the entrance is through double farm gates, across a cattle grid. Although the club celebrated its centenary in 2006, this has not always been the entrance, indeed the course has only been sited at High Studdon since 1992. Prior to this Allendale Golf Club could be found at The Portgate Links, Broadwood Hall and, most recently, Thornley Gate. In the early years, visitors would arrive by railway on the single-track line running between Allendale and Hexham which opened on 1st March 1869 and closed to passengers in September 1930. For twenty four years this would be how many golfers found their way to the town and its hotels, the most imposing and best remembered being the Heatherlea. Every August Bank Holiday Monday golfers still compete for the Heatherlea Cup, the Allendale Open with a fine trophy dating back to 1912. There are other connections;

4

Tommy Shield owned the Heatherlea near its end while his son John was closely involved with establishing the new course at High Studdon and was the greenkeeper until 2004. There are many connections in this close and isolated community, just don't expect to commit a misdemeanour and get away with it; the crime will be solved by the court of public opinion in the King's Head and the Golden Lion that same evening, the suspect found guilty and the gallows erected in the village square the following morning. If this view of a 'Wicker Man' community appears overstated then I recommend a trip to the village on New Year's Eve. Men in strange garb parade the streets with burning tar barrels perched on their heads prior to launching the flaming cauldrons on to a bonfire in the middle of the square, perilously close to nearby buildings. In this safety-conscious, risk-averse modern world it is a joy that such traditions survive, nevertheless, it is an odd and disturbing spectacle.

Grand hotels once serviced a large number of tourists for there was a time when both the town and its golf course were a popular holiday destination for Tynesiders. This was particularly so during Glasgow and Edinburgh weeks when residents at the coast would rent out their homes to the marauding Scots and then escape to the peace of the Allen Valley. The Heatherlea was famous for its dinner gong, hickory clubs stacked in the hallway, unending stairs and the smell of food rising from the kitchens and filling the dark hallways; it is now converted to flats. The Hotspur is a private house and The Dale, formerly a Temperance House, is abandoned and empty, along with temperance and most of the Methodist chapels that demanded it.

The demise of the passenger rail service was brought about by a competing two-hourly bus service from Newcastle, calling at Hexham and Haydon Bridge on the way to the centre of Allendale. The regularity and convenience of a bus which linked town centres and took no longer than the train, had dire consequences for rail passenger numbers

particularly when the railway station was over a mile from the town centre at the southern end of another village, Catton. As freight traffic also dwindled over the next twenty years, the line was finally closed in November 1950 and the rails lifted, pre-empting Beeching's axe. The photograph is from the Allendale Golf Club Centenary Collection and shows golfers waiting at the railway station.

Almost everyone now arrives by car and, whilst a bus service still runs from Hexham, passengers rarely carry golf clubs. Driving into the course at High Studdon, you are immediately presented with a view of the high moors, Dryburn, Acton and Longwell, stretching south up the Allen Valley towards Knockshield, Hartley and, eventually, the town of Allenheads. This high terrain, rising above 1,640 feet, frames the course to the south and west and dominates first impressions. You are left in no doubt that you have reached a vast and empty landscape. On most days you will be almost entirely alone except for distant sheep.

6

Cattle grids, honesty boxes, damp air, empty fairways and lightly trodden greens, this is the essence of *Golf in the Wild*. This is Allendale. It is a miracle that the golf club and others like it continue to exist at all. In a remote place with a diminishing community and small catchment area, the membership is constrained by geographic, social and economic circumstance. And then there is the belief amongst 'serious' golfers that somehow a 9-hole course is not for them; they have no idea what they are missing.

In the centenary year three local professionals were invited to challenge the course and break par, something which had never been done before. Two out of the three hit their tee shot from the first out of bounds into the adjacent field. Despite this they soon appreciated the pleasures of this course on the side of a mountain; one was moved to observe '*it can be a bit of a shock getting the ball in the hole. Being short, the course has to protect itself and it does that very well ... the course is a great antidote to every new 7,000-yard course being designed for slam-bang hitters and with the scenery, it's a perfect place to come and play golf.*' They did not break par.

Limited members, small numbers of visitors and no capital reserves, the annual turnover has never exceeded £50,000, a small fraction of the costs associated with other even moderately sized clubs. So how is the course always so well presented, how are the greens playable throughout the year, in short, how does this miracle happen? Because the members love it, because a small band of enthusiastic volunteers recognise the value of their course and are prepared to dedicate hours of their time to ensure its survival. There are endless tasks associated with the running of a golf club and yet there is but one employee, the greenkeeper, by necessity a gifted *Jack of all trades*. However, there are benefits to these straitened circumstances. The course is never busy, the membership is never high, limited numbers mean that almost everyone knows everyone else; it is friendly.

7

The toffee-nosed element from the well-heeled club does not exist, the tightly packed fairways of the urban club are unheard of and the brashness of the corporate and hotel clubs is nowhere to be seen – *'money doesn't talk, it swears'.*[4] This is always a gentle and welcoming place, except perhaps for the weather, which can be a touch demanding when the wind blows.

The picture of gentlemen golfers putting out is from the course at Broadwood Hall, probably taken not long after the club was formed at the turn of the last century (from the Allendale Golf Club Centenary Collection). The farm buildings in the background, which still exist today, are at 955 feet, a slightly lower altitude than the current clubhouse. Thornley Gate was just down the road from Broadwood Hall and even Portgate Links near the town centre was well above 800 feet. Golf at these altitudes is always testing. Consequently, Allendale golfers have always been obliged to play the elements as well as the course, and it is evident as soon as you arrive at High Studdon that the present-day course is no exception. Prevailing winds charge down the first fairway straight into the face of the first tee and power the turbine; it could not be sited in a more ideal location. All of the trees on the course bend in the same direction, but there are days when the wind blows from the north east and the average golfer might just reach the first in two, although peering at the distant flag from the tee you might question if that could ever be true. Immediately to the left of the tee and for over two hundred yards, are the galleries – disinterested Hexham Blackfaces munching in the out-of-bounds. Although two out of three centenary professionals planted their drives amongst the sheep, undeterred, the third drove straight down the fairway edging the field along the entire flight of the ball. There was never any suggestion that a professional would take the safer line, never a hint of concern. My game is all about concern, a state of mind I mistake for concentration.

All in all, Allendale's first, *Long Reach,* is a tough opener, especially into the prevailing wind. The lower half of the green slopes towards you which helps those who cannot spin the ball, but the over eager go long at their peril as beyond the green there be dragons. To be more accurate, in winter it will be roe deer grazing out of sight in the dip behind the first green. At the merest hint of an approaching golfer they launch themselves in startled flight towards higher ground, the third tee and beyond. Roe deer will generally not graze in a field used by livestock, preferring to consume 'clean' grass. This makes the golf course a Michelin-starred destination for *Capreolus capreolus* and probably explains why many saplings struggle to survive beyond knee high. Nevertheless, there is still a mix of mature trees across the course, but none obscure the horizon. Turn to the north west at the first green and on a clear day the views stretch to the Cheviots and the Scottish Borders. And time should be taken to look. *Golf in the Wild* is about slow time, the land, silence and escape. I am not convinced that you need share the experience. I am of the opinion that such places can be enjoyed on your own and in your own time.

James Bartholomew writing in *Slightly Foxed – The Reader's Quarterly*,[5] makes these observations on two P. G. Wodehouse golfing stories and the lone golfer playing in the twilight of a wintry day:

> *'There he is in the dark, distant part of the course taking twelve shots at every hole. But he still keeps at it. He fails and fails again but he keeps trying. It is only a game, but he loves it. And that in a few sentences, is life. Ridiculous? Well, in life we flog our guts out and try to achieve things or find true love or just get the kitchen clean and finally it all ends in nothingness. In a hundred years, none of us will be here and hardly anyone will remember us.'*

The ninth stanza of Gray's *Elegy Written in a Country Churchyard* [6] says the same, but more succinctly, and should remind us that missing the 3-foot putt in the monthly medal is of no consequence, neither was sinking that 30 footer the week before:

> *The boasts of heraldry, the pomp of pow'r,*
> *And all that beauty, and all that wealth e'er gave,*
> *Await alike the inevitable hour,*
> *The paths of glory lead but to the grave.*

We are social animals and perhaps the company of a close friend who shares your passion or a non-playing partner happy to amble in paradise would be preferable to avoid dark thoughts of mortality. At a stretch you could make it a three-ball but never four – much too crowded. Better a well-trained dog; it is easy to imagine a black lab sitting patiently at your bag between shots although, to avoid frustration, it is probably best to avoid retrievers. By contrast, is there a more depressing sight than coaches in the car park and overly serious, logo bejewelled golfers crowding the first tee?

The tenth, *Centennial*, shares the same green as the first but, like six others on the back nine, starts from a different tee box. So it is with the second and twelfth, *Penny Black* and *Penny Red*; the names pay homage to the *Postage Stamp* at Troon. From this narrow elevated green, invisible from both tee boxes, it is a short walk to the third, *Chimney*, and the highest point on the course at 1,136 feet. Walk to the small copse of beech trees in the corner, look over the wall and the Allen Valley stretches before you in all its grandeur. Returning to the tee box and 100 feet below is the green. If you think you need to play a provisional, play it before you set off down the hill, the return climb would sap your energy for the rest of the round.

Everything about this hole is on the vertical plane, a portrait rather than landscape view. The approach to the green is framed by trees right and left and the eye is drawn upwards to Flow Moss and the Allen Mill chimney, after which the hole is named; the top of another chimney, set further back, is also visible on clear days. The chimneys and their flues were built in 1808 to vent sulphur and arsenic, a by-product of the Allen Mill lead ore smelting process which first started operating in 1692. The Allen Valley was once the richest source of lead in Britain. The smelt mill down near the railway station has largely gone but there are some significant remnants including stone storage bunkers, a condensing chamber, silver smelter and a flue opening. The flue system runs from Allen Mill to the chimneys with some impressive statistics; at their widest and highest they are over 6 feet and 24 feet respectively and run for over 2 miles. While some stretches have collapsed much remains and a walk to the chimneys allows a closer inspection of one of the best preserved flue systems in England, now a Scheduled Monument.

Lead ore can contain significant concentrations of silver and this was recognised in the construction of the flues; doors gave access to enable the silver to be scraped or brushed from the lining; is this where

11

the phrase 'daft as a brush' derives from, the sulphur and arsenic having the same effect as mercury on a mad hatter. The lead brought the railways, the railways brought the people and the people played golf.

From the third tee keep the idea of chimneys in your mind and try floating a ball down the stack and onto the green; you can come up short on the bank but, in the summer, the ball may bounce off the slope and over the back of the green, requiring the use of crampons to retrieve it. In the winter the ball will simply stop dead. The approach to the same green from the twelfth tee on the back nine is wholly different and characterises how the local course designers cleverly extracted the best from the land available. Offset to the right and further down the hill, *Crow's Nest* invites an ace. It is known as the Northern Rock shot; pitch the ball to the left and use the run on the bank to gather the ball to the hole. I offer no apologies to Adam Applegarth; I am still waiting for his.

Down the hill from the third green are the parallel fourth and thirteenth fairways, *Throstle* and *Isaac's Trail*. The *Throstle* is named after the recently renovated cottage on the other side of the Allenheads Road; the story is that the new owner is married to a Russian ballet dancer. The removal of the Iron Curtain had wonderful consequences – in the space of a generation, an entire gender has transformed from the 15-stone weightlifters of my youth into a nation of stunning models, ballerinas and graceful, if grunting, tennis players; it makes you grateful for Glasnost, pleased about Perestroika.

The parallel thirteenth, *Isaac's Trail*, is named after the themed walk that runs adjacent to the lower reaches of the course. Isaac Holden was an itinerant nineteenth century tea seller and philanthropist. A former lead miner, he walked from his Allendale grocery shop selling his wares in Sinderhope, Nenthead, Alston, Kirkhaugh, Ninebanks and Whitfield. The route celebrates his philanthropic endeavours which included raising money to buy a horse-drawn hearse for the parish of West Allen thus allowing the locals to bring out their dead in some style.

The two fairways slope perilously towards the Allenheads Road along their entire length. The green does the same. Reaching the green is tough, getting the ball in the hole even tougher. The fifth and fourteenth fairways share the same tee, *The Hagg*, which starts the return to higher ground. *The Hagg* is a seventeenth century former farmstead located due west from the tee box and not a reference to the Scottish Play. However, when the weather turns and the winds whip in from the north east, you could mistake this landscape for some blasted heath. The gnarled hawthorns bend to ease the strain from the prevailing winds and, while it seems unlikely they have an ambition to reach Dunsinane Hill, they do appear to be making a concerted effort to reach Hexham; a hooked ball in a prevailing westerly will attempt to follow.

Halfway up the hill the sixth and fifteenth, *Hawk's Drift* and *Perdition* head west into the prevailing winds. *Hawk's Drift* is a moderate stroke index par 4 but, due to improving club technology, the old men in blazers (Northumberland Union of Golf Clubs) insisted that the course had to be lengthened in order to maintain the current Standard Scratch Score. The sixth competition white tees have therefore been moved back some 150 yards and the hole made the par 5, which any self-respecting golf course demands. The additional length changes the character of the hole and suddenly a gully and line of trees that dissect the fairway are brought into play on the second shot. Inevitably, this leads to complaints; it just takes one sweetly struck rising fairway shot to clip a high branch and all hell and fury is brought down upon that den of scoundrels, the Committee. I choose to believe this is not personal, instead it is like most collective bodies, an amorphous bureaucratic mass upon which we vent our ire; reason and quiet solicitude have little effect on our desire to blame others. This is inevitable and part of the modern human condition. The problems arise when these same bureaucracies attempt the sincere and personal; there are many examples from history including the modern obsession with apology but this one is personal.

*

My great uncle Billy was my maternal grandfather's younger brother who served in the Royal Flying Corps during the Great War. He survived the conflict but died in the final hours, struck down by Spanish flu. *'La Grippe Espagnole'* killed more people than were lost during the entire 1914–1918 war. It has been cited as the most devastating epidemic in world history, killing more people in a single year than died during the four years of the Black Death.

His distraught parents, my maternal great grandparents, received this acknowledgement of a life taken too early:

> *The King commands me to assure you of the true sympathy of His Majesty and the Queen in your sorrow. He whose loss you mourn died in the noblest of causes. His Country will be ever grateful to him for the sacrifice he has made for Freedom and Justice.*

An unthinking example of disconnected bureaucracy, it fails to acknowledge who '*He*' is, while succumbing to flu is somehow deemed a noble cause rather than the tragic chance act of nature it really was. The standard letter is 'signed' (printed) Winston S. Churchill, Secretary of State for the Royal Air Force (the RFC became the RAF on 1st April 1918). Billy died on 5th November 1918 aged twenty five and was buried six days later on a day heavy with symbolism, November 11th, Armistice Day. His funeral was marked with military honours at Andover Cemetery in the presence of his mother, father, *'chums and superior officers'* and his fiancée, Miss Coombes. Miss Coombes and Billy, the great-aunt and uncle I never had. My grandfather, Fred, was still half a world away in Egypt and, given the communications of the day, almost certainly unaware of his loss.

The King commands me to assure you of the true sympathy of His Majesty and The Queen in your sorrow.

He whose loss you mourn died in the noblest of causes. His Country will be ever grateful to him for the sacrifice he has made for Freedom and Justice.

Secretary of State for the Royal Air Force.

*

The fifteenth, *Perdition,* heads for the same hole but from an elevated tee some 60 yards back from the shorter sixth. The extra distance again brings the same gully and line of trees into play and makes for a devilish par 4. Perdition: a state of eternal punishment and damnation into which a sinful and impenitent person passes after death. Get this hole wrong and you can experience the afterlife, first hand. There is a story of a recently deceased golfer who finds himself on the most beautiful course imaginable. At the clubhouse there are rows and rows of shining irons and dazzling woods to choose from. He happily surmises that a fortuitous mistake has been made by the recording angel and that he must be in heaven after all. Then a caddie appears as if from nowhere. A slight figure with narrow red eyes and an unfortunate body odour, he shuffles to the golfer's side and whispers in his ear – *'welcome to Perdition Golf Club, there are no balls'.*

The seventh and sixteenth, *The Crossing*, share the same tee and destination. I had wanted the hole to be called *The Styx* but my morbid fascination with the dark side found no support on the Committee. Like *Perdition*, it can be devilish. If you wished to distil Allendale Golf Course into one hole, this could be it. *The Crossing* is not the signature hole, that comes next, but it has all the right ingredients: trees invading your peripheral vision, a sizeable but invisible gully, a sloping fairway and danger left, right and through the green. Hit the ball high, long and straight and it is uncomplicated, but how many of us can do that to order. The hole also demonstrates why only buggies with advanced traction control systems would be suitable in such a landscape; in the space of a few steps, the course drops and rises 20 feet such that the best all-terrain vehicle would struggle to stay upright, as does the golf trolley, as does the average biped.

Allendale and Catton have close associations, not least because the Allendale railway station was inconveniently located in this small village to the north of the Allen River. Throughout the summer the members compete for the Catton Trophy in the club's knockout championship. The only dogleg on the course, it was an imaginative wag who suggested calling it the *Catton Dogleg*. The long hitter can take the shortcut over the pine trees to the left, the moderate hitter over the beech trees in the centre, the sensible hitter heads for the fairway to the right and the unreliable hitter has a choice of three, but only one is safe. The green was unique for being the only one which hosted an array of bunkers but these were removed in 2012 due to their odd positioning and the habit of local rabbits to treat them as their personal sand pits. The maintenance overheads were disproportionately high so the Committee took the decision to have them grassed over. Somebody, somewhere, sometime will be cursing that den of scoundrels again.

The approach to the same hole from the seventeenth tee, across *The Grand Canyon*, is an altogether different proposition. This par 3 is

Allendale's signature hole and a work of genius. The elevated tee box sits on a natural promontory while the green is 149 yards across the *Canyon*, no great distance but many a topped ball has put an end to a promising medal round. Down in the *Canyon* there are conifers, rabbits, the greenkeeper's shed, a pond, a stream, rare orchids and broken dreams in the shape of lost golf balls. Forster Milburn (1935 – 2008) had much to do with the design of the course and this hole in particular. It is fitting that a bench with magnificent views to the Cheviots, marks both his passing and his hole-in-one in 2007, at this, his best creation.

Finally the ninth, *Studdon Straight*, a par 3 and the eighteenth, *Last Gasp* brings you back to the clubhouse. From the ninth tee, the hole looks reasonably straightforward but plays long due to some rising ground in front of the green; it is called the lie of the land. From the eighteenth tee at the bottom of the hill, nothing of the course can be seen, only the top of the turbine, the marker post and the distant fairways to the west. A moderate drive could end up in the clubhouse window or in the one remaining bunker which sits in the centre of the fairway – the product of an anarchic greenkeeper, long since departed. The climb back to level ground is the final exertion required before sinking the last putt and retiring to the nineteenth hole.

If you are lucky, there will be a soft breeze and the turbine will spin gently against a deep blue sky. Sheep will be grazing on the fells; the lonesome call of the curlew will fill the silent air; a hare will be seen scurrying down the first. In the clubhouse the greenkeepers will be eating their lunch and will be persuaded to open the bar whilst in the background the click of a driver will sound from the first tee where the only other players have just arrived for a friendly two ball. The high moors will be lit by a clean bright light, framed by the clubhouse windows, your heart will lift. This is surely golf heaven. Allendale is the perfect introduction to *Golf in the Wild*.

Notes

1. From *Save the Life of My Child,* Simon and Garfunkel's *Bookends* album, re-leased April 1968. One of the early concept albums, the first side of the vinyl LP has a musically unified cradle-to-grave theme, which begins and ends with the *Bookends Theme.* The book begins and ends with quotes from this album.

2. Quoted with the permission of Julie Riso, travel writer and blogger, *The literary journeys of J. D. Riso*: *Wish I Were Here* – julieriso.wordpress.com.

3. Ordnance Survey 1:50 000 scale Map 87, Hexham and Haltwhistle.

4. *It's Alright, Ma (I'm Only Bleeding)*, Bob Dylan, from the *Bringing it all Back Home* album, released 1965.

5. Quoted with the permission of James Bartholomew. First published under the title *If at first....*in Slightly Foxed No. 27 Autumn 2010 - The P. G. Wodehouse golfing stories - *The Clicking of Cuthbert* (1922) and *Heart of a Goof* (1926) (Bartholomew, 2010).

6. Extract from *Elegy Written in a Country Churchyard*, Thomas Gray, completed in 1750 and first published in 1751.

The Borders

The open road! The dusty highway!
Come! I'll show you the world
The adventures of Ichabod and Mr
Toad – Walt Disney, 1949

I confess that I have an unhealthy appetite for cars with more than a hint of the irresponsible. Hot hatches, Japanese coupés, English sports cars with a heritage have all passed through my hands. My philosophy is that cars are not just vehicles for transport, the more they are practical, the less they are desirable. Cars are jewellery, cars are to be desired, cars are to be coveted and driven hard. There is joy in sweeping curves and the sound of an engine 'on song'. People carriers, diesel engines and SUVs are the work of the devil. My own choice of vehicle might be considered bizarre in this age of sky-high petrol prices and environmental concerns, but, as I remember one motoring journalist astutely observing, the Wankel engine goes like stink, sounds like it is lubricated by cream and always raises a laugh. Importantly, the boot is big enough for a full set of golf clubs (but not a trolley). In Toad-like fashion, this desire is only surpassed by a recently acquired passion for two-wheeled transport, but I have yet to find a Ducati that will accommodate even a modest collection of irons.

I have some green credentials, having been closely associated with the installation of the wind turbine at Allendale Golf Club, but the truth is that I am more Jeremy Clarkson than James Lovelock, more Ghia than Gaia. The journey from green to tee is therefore central to this book, satisfying a desire for both open fairways and open roads. The journey north becomes progressively more spectacular, such that between the vernal and autumnal equinoxes it is a journey into the light. Put your foot to the floor and enjoy the ride. The recommended route tries to avoid motorways, dual carriageways and major conurbations. Do not use a sat-nav, get out a folding roadmap, best suited for examining, unfolded, across the warm bonnet of a rag top or hot coupé. The next stop is Selkirk – 75 miles in approximately two hours.

Find your way back down the hill to the B6295 and turn right towards Allendale town centre. Drive through the town keeping to the main road, heading north towards Catton and sign-posted Hexham. The road to Catton becomes the B6303 and the B6304 briefly before joining the B6305 at Branchend. At this point the road has slowly climbed to 958 feet and on a clear day, Northumberland is spread before you. Carry on towards Hexham with the race course to your right and another wind turbine on your left at West Nubbock Farm.

The B6305 eventually arrives at Hexham at traffic lights opposite the Fox Inn. The navigator's challenge from here is to make a connection with the A68 without venturing onto the major east-west dual carriageway, the A69. This is simply achieved by crossing Hexham Bridge and turning immediate right along Ferry Road which leads to Corbridge. It is odd to reflect that had history taken a different course, this bridge, dating from 1793, might not exist at all, at least in its current form. If, during the Second World War, Germany had decided to invade England from the north then all of the bridges along the North Tyne would have been sacrificed – it is said that holes for dynamite were drilled in every span of every bridge and that these holes are still visible today, although I confess I have yet to find evidence. A couple of miles along Ferry Road the name changes to Corchester Lane and on the rising ground to the left the John Dobson-designed Beaufront Castle comes into view; in the event of a Nazi invasion this was designated the headquarters for the Battle of the Tyne. Assuming the attack was expected from the north, it seems bizarre that battle HQ should be sited north of the defensive line, the River Tyne. Perhaps it is just as well the Nazis never planted their feet on Northumberland soil, the Battle of Beaufront Castle may have been a short-lived and tragic event.

It is understandable that for schoolboys brought up in the 1950s, the Second World War holds a certain fascination. For our parents and older siblings it was immediate history while my grandparents had survived not one but two major European conflicts. In the streets we played Cowboys and Indians but we also played Tommies and Jerries fed by a constant diet of war stories on film, television, in comics and books. We were also raised by a generation with a more reasoned attitude towards mortality; life was never considered cheap, but so many had perished so recently that when tragedy struck there was a measured response – accidents happen, mistakes are made, to err is human. The 1955 Le Mans tragedy is a case in point; eighty three spectators and one driver dead and many more injured, one of the worst sporting accidents in history but the race continued to its end.

At the end of Corchester Lane, on the outskirts of Corbridge, turn left and head north. In a short distance you drive under the A69 where this local minor road becomes the A68, a monster. The severe dips and blind crests can be alarming during the day and scary at night when headlights illuminate the sky and not the road, so accident rates are high. Once north of West Woodburn, the road becomes more inviting, joining the A696 at Elishaw and proceeding north to the Scottish Border. My teenage obsession with hallowed racing tarmac has never left me and I still search out echoes of the past in roads of the present.

*

I was born in a nursing home in the unromantically named *Navigation Road*, just outside Altrincham. This is a stop on the Altrincham to Manchester railway line which, before conversion to a tram system, used to terminate at Manchester Central, now a Convention Complex. For much of its length the line follows the course of the Bridgewater Canal although by the time they reach Altrincham they have gone their separate ways. One of my earliest compulsive recitals was the station names on what was originally called the Manchester, South Junction and Altrincham Railway – no concerns for snappy domain names in those days; today a branding and marketing company would charge a fortune to come up with a one-word label significant only for being unique and meaningless.

Seven stations north from Altrincham was Warwick Road, the stop for Old Trafford, home to football and cricket. For those with limited name association capabilities, the it has since been rechristened Old Trafford, which it is not. Journeys along this line feature large in my internal landscape, my geography of the soul, when Manchester was the centre of my small universe; when steam was king, trainspotting at Manchester Exchange and Victoria stations; Manchester Free Trade Hall for concerts – Tom Paxton, Simon and Garfunkel (not the Hallé); big city cinemas to impress first dates; the guitar and music shops on Oxford Road; Kendals' sale to be miserably kitted out in 'smart' clothes and, yes, occasional test cricket and football matches but my theatre of dreams, my Shangri-La, was elsewhere. I was seduced by the velvet tones of Raymond Baxter and grainy images from BBC 405-line outside broadcasts; for as long as I can remember I have been obsessed with racing.

I feel a certain affinity with the motor racing journalist Nigel Roebuck; both Cheshire boys of a similar and certain age, we spent a large part of our teenage years trackside at Oulton Park watching our helmeted heroes go by. He went onto achieve what I only aspired to; I still have copies of my early 'race reports', evidence of intent if not talent. This is a short extract from his *Reflections* column[1] in *Motor Sport*:

Hard as it may be to believe in 2012, when the enchanting Mr Rooney trousers £220,000 a week, there was a time when sportsmen – of all kinds – frequently struggled to make ends meet. The Manchester United team of the mid to late 1950s – the legendary 'Busby Babes', was emphatically the best in the land but it was hardly reflected in the players' wage packets. One of them, tragically lost at Munich in February 1958, was a patient of my father and told him one day of the great celebration at the club for the Captain, Roger Byrne, had acquired a Morris Minor, thus becoming the team's first player to own a car. United's bonus scheme was simple: £2 for a win, a quid for a draw.

Another northerner, Dodie Smith, tells the story of her early life in Manchester in her autobiography, *Look Back With Love*. A playwright and novelist, her best-known work is *The Hundred and One Dalmatians*, written out of sheer irritation at Enid Blyton's success. I was drawn to the book because she grew up in Old Trafford in the early twentieth century when it was still a pleasant suburb before becoming the blackened building, smoke and fog landscape of my 1950s childhood; it would be very hard to imagine Old Trafford as a pleasant suburb, even more so then, than now. Dodie moved away from Manchester in 1910, so there is no mention of the football ground, United only moving to Old Trafford that same year. However, there is brief mention of the cricket ground and the nearby dusty road on which her grandfather would draw ships with his walking stick. He was perhaps inspired by those he saw travelling across fields near their house; the Manchester Ship Canal was in sight of their Old Trafford home, Kingston House (eventually demolished to make way for a new railway).

It is a gentle story of a gentle upbringing on the eve of great change. There is an illuminating tale of a car journey in a dark red De Dion Bouton from Old Trafford to Tenby when such a trip would be a rare and grand adventure:

Those were the days of dusty roads; as soon as we left the suburbs of Manchester the hedges were powdered white and a great white cloud followed us. Whenever we saw another car approaching us, we stuffed handkerchiefs into our mouths, covered our faces with our hands and ducked, but even so the dust was suffocating. As I came up for air I always cast an admiring glance at Uncle Bertie, upright, indomitable and be-goggled at the wheel, his pipe with its patent spark-preventing lid clenched between his teeth. Not for him to duck from dust clouds and, as the hours wore on, his face, moustache and cap grew white as any miller's.

I am slightly perplexed as to why the roads around Manchester would be throwing up white dust, this being something I have always associated with the chalk uplands of Hampshire and Dorset; indeed, travel the minor roads of those counties today and there is still evidence of chalk cuttings beneath ancient tree-shrouded byways. Maybe chalk was the forerunner of tarmac; maybe memories play tricks.

*

Just William, my teenage partner in crime attended a grammar school which bizarrely sent pupils home on a Tuesday afternoon, but, as penance, they were required to attend on Saturday mornings. His father, Douglas, was an art lecturer at Manchester University but his real passions were small-scale engineering, Colin Chapman and Jim Clark. A member of the Lancashire and Cheshire car club, he rarely missed an event at Oulton Park. One happy Saturday he took me along for company and from that moment I was hooked. Two smells will transport me back to '*the happy highways where I went and cannot come again* '[2] (A. E. Houseman): steam engines and hot Castrol R. They should be bottled by Giorgio Armani; they would command a high price. There are stretches of the A68 north of West Woodburn which resemble Belgium's classic Grand Prix circuit, pure Spa-Francorchamps: long sweeping downhill bends, tall pines, rapidly emerging vistas. Like Spa, there is always a strong possibility of rain. It is not difficult to imagine a Lola T70 Mk III let loose on this Northumberland tarmac, threading the needle's eye at 180mph, a Chevrolet V-8 thundering towards the northern light. This was a car I sketched on the cover of many a school exercise book, the perfect shape, the perfect mid-engined configuration, radiator to the front, the engine in front of the rear wheel line, two seats in the middle. There are many other examples from the same era; powerful, fragile cars offering minimal protection to the fearsome professional race drivers of the late 1960s. The version in the picture was driven by New Zealander, Paul Hawkins, approaching Lodge Corner at Oulton Park on a very wet afternoon, in practice for the RAC Tourist Trophy, 25th May 1969. I stood happy in the rain, clicked my Dad's 35mm Werra camera and captured the monster, nose-dipped under braking, hunting a dry line.

Later that miserable May afternoon, that same rain would prompt Hawkins to shelter in Little Budworth church opposite the pub where he was staying. His minister father wondered if he had a premonition of his *'approaching confrontation with God'*.[3] The next morning, race day dawned brighter, spring had returned to the Cheshire countryside. Chasing the leaders on the ragged edge, 'Hawkeye' slid wide at Esso Bend and died in a petrol and magnesium inferno. An all-too-familiar sight in those dangerous days – a pall of black smoke climbed high into a clear Spring sky marking the hour and the place.

The circuit fell silent as the cars peeled into the pit lane such that, on this occasion, the race was abandoned. A tragic end to a heroic man, but surely '*one crowded hour of glorious life is worth an age without a name*' – Sir Walter Scott, Sheriff of Selkirkshire.[4]

*

The A68 hugs the western perimeter of the Otterburn firing ranges, the largest in the country, before passing a series of interconnected reservoirs built at the beginning of the last century to provide drinking water to Newcastle and Gateshead. This is Redesdale and once the country home of Lord Redesdale, father to the infamous Mitford Sisters, a family who will appear later in this story in the unlikeliest of remote places.

At Carter Bar the A68 climbs to 1,371 feet, crosses into Scotland and, on a clear day, this separate land is spread out before you; it will be some distance before the landscape matches the recently travelled wild stretches of north Northumberland. Just beyond the summit take the first left, the A6088 sign-posted Hawick, thus avoiding a series of speed cameras which welcome the unwary to Scotland along the A68. The descent from Carter Bar is surrounded by new and old mono-culture tree plantations, mostly of non-native conifers. The negative impact on native wild life is well documented and the switch to native broad leafs cannot come soon enough, but in the meantime, the harvesting of such trees leaves a patched landscape which resembles a war zone.

The landscape softens towards Bonchester Bridge before eventually reaching Hawick and the A7. From here follow the signs to Selkirk where before long the 783-foot transmitter tower, sited next to Lindean Loch, comes into view. Built in 1961 to bring ITV's 405 lines to south east Scotland, it was not converted to 625 until 1985. Imagine the tragic images transmitted from this tower to burn into a black and white collective memory: Dallas, 22nd November 1963; Memphis, 4th April 1968, and three days later, Hockenheim, 7th April 1968. A second transmitter at Ashkirk appears on the skyline as you approach Selkirk and the golf course; at night both are lit up by bright red lights from base to tip, providing a festive atmosphere to the countryside throughout the year; a celebration of bad news.

The golf course has a narrow entrance next to a white cottage on the right and is easily missed. When you do, turn around at the crossroads before the garage and there is the golf course facing you on *The Hill*; from here it looks as if you will need dozens of spare balls.

Notes

1. From the magazine *Motor Sport* Vol. 88, N. 10. – October 2012 edition, Nigel Roebuck – *Reflections* column.

2. Extract from *A Shropshire Lad,* 1896 – A. E. Houseman (1859-1936).

3. The story of Paul Hawkins' father is told in Ivan McLeod's book *Hawkeye*, which dismisses the late conversion – it was simply somewhere to go to get out of the rain (McLeod, 2003).

4. Sir Walter Scott, more famous as a poet and historical novelist, he was also Sheriff of Selkirkshire from 1799 to 1832 – the next destination on this journey.

Selkirk & Innerleithen

You drank beer, you played golf, you watched football – WE EVOLVED! Frank Zappa

The entrance is modest, the course sharing its driveway with a white but'n'ben house which sits end onto the main road. Golf has been played on Selkirk Hill since 1893 so this is well-trodden turf. There is a steep climb to the first tee box, from where a distant marker post hints at the right line for *Briar Bank* and a journey into the unknown, at least for the uninitiated. The clubhouse nestles in the lee of the Hill where just down the road, the town is creeping up the A7, its extremities marked by the unsympathetic primary colours of a petrol station. This apart, the views are glorious – splendour, splendour everywhere. The distant wind turbines are static, blades at rest on their shoulders as though presenting arms. I have picked a good day to play the course, a day which left me wanting more; that is the best litmus test, when you just cannot get enough. Each round of golf is an adventure with its own narrative and, by its end, another unique set of excuses. I am adept in such matters.

I was born to the mother of invention. In a tight corner, looking for an excuse, offering a judgement on someone's character, providing reassurance, any of these and Peg had a quick, wicked imagination; a compulsive desire to construct an alternative to the real world; a parallel universe that more accurately supported her opinions and prejudice. In her decline she came to inhabit a place somewhere between the two. She was an Alan Bennett untold story.

Giving a lift to an ageing nervous spinster she would try to inspire confidence – *'don't worry my dear, I drove lorries for the Land Army during the war'*. This of course was wholly untrue, for Peggy was married in 1943 aged nineteen and moved from working in an Andover shop to Manchester, where my father worked in a reserved occupation at Trafford Park. She fell pregnant with my sister almost immediately and gave birth in March 1944. Whenever my teenage sister was being particularly difficult she would be reminded how, in a bizarre twist of responsibility, *'I carried you through the Blitz'*. Even to a less than generous younger brother this seemed harsh. It was also not true, the Manchester Christmas Blitz took place in December 1940. A penchant for the untruth was combined with some strong opinions. There was my first serious girlfriend who was subject to continuous public inquiry – *'That girl is a gold digger, she is just after your money – But Mum, I don't have any! Well if you did she would be!'*

Half-truths, half-baked ideas and of course a fully baked imagination, she was a master of the unthinking opinion. *'I like Jews but not their businessmen'*– this to a couple she had just met on holiday. They were called Cohen and sold carpets up Shude Hill in Manchester. They remained close friends for the rest of their lives which says much for 'Jewish businessmen' and little for our Peg. Oy Vey, she never even bought a carpet.

Mostly, she worried, a state of mind she mistook for wisdom and a life philosophy based on *'always assume the worst'*, no matter how small the threat. When Dad retired they moved to a small village near Sherborne in Dorset and on one of my visits I went into town and bought a well-used US ex-Army coat, actually a lined parka complete with insignia. The shop was opposite Sherborne School and I suspect they sold well to rebellious adolescents, a very familiar club to whom I still paid my dues. I was delighted with my bargain purchase and proudly wore it home – Peg was immediately alarmed *'Robin, you can't possibly wear that, you will catch Venereal Disease!'*.

Peg would have been at home in a clubhouse for we all have the desire to invent a parallel world; the putts that could have dropped but didn't, the balls that vanished on the fairway, the chips that kissed the pin then disappeared into a bunker. But for these ungodly interventions that round of ten over could have been 5 under. Almost all television interviews with professional golfers will demand that this is the only subject for discussion; *what might have been*. By contrast, the winner will conclude that the apparently random was the inevitable, the intended. Thanks will be passed to all and sundry and in the case of North Americans, it will be attributed to faith and divine intervention as though God didn't have enough on his plate; a strangely, oversentimental race, out of kilter with their predilection for firearms. Since the assassination of Kennedy, more Americans died by gunfire in their own country than perished on foreign battlefields throughout the whole of the twentieth century.

*

As I square up to *The Hill*, I am already contemplating my wayward statistics and preparing more excuses.

The clubhouse was officially opened on 21st May 1924 and a picture hung high in the entrance lobby commemorates the event; the juniors, gents and ladies are lined up in six rows, evidence of a thriving and proud club. Adjacent to this photograph is a collection of portraits of the club champions dating from 1893 to 1903, all taken by the local photographer, Robert D Clapperton. His original *Daylight Photographic Studio* can be found in Scotts Place, Selkirk, not far from the town centre. Dating from 1867, it is now a small family-owned museum located in what is believed to be the last surviving genuine daylight photographic premises in the UK.

It is a fascinating unchanged place haunted by the ghosts of a thousand sepia sitters, forever breathing the faint odour of developer and hypo. Most of the champions' photographs were taken in this studio each with similar props and backdrops. The champion's shield[1] is an impressive trophy awarded on four consecutive years from 1896 to John Hardie and then again in 1904. This started life as the *Border Challenge Trophy*, a team inter-club championship dating from 1890. From the outset it was agreed that, should any of the competing clubs win the trophy in three consecutive years, they would retain it in perpetuity. It has never left Selkirk and was awarded to the club champion until 1966; it is now on permanent display in the clubhouse lounge with eight unused spaces; eight men denied immortality.

Armed with Cobra's latest technology, driving from the first tee is not too daunting. When you reach the crest of the hill you realise that this is a generous fairway and the second to the green an inviting prospect; initial impressions of tight fairways and punishing heather begin to fade. What an altogether different prospect this course must have been with hickory clubs from 1893. The current layout actually dates from 1924 when it was revised by Willie Park junior, Open Champion in 1887 and 1889 at Musselburgh, the world's oldest playing golf course. A designer and manufacturer of golf equipment, course designer and writer, 'Young Willie' was one of the top professionals of his generation. His long game was sometimes unreliable but on and around the greens he was supreme – *'A man who can putt is a match for anyone'* – he said that. *'A man who cannot putt will suffer sleep deprivation'* – I said that. Suffering from ill health, he returned from America to die in Scotland in 1925 at the age of 61. Redesigning the course on Selkirk Hill was his final act.

Looking at a layout of the original course (1893–1923), the current ninth green is on or near the old first and the second up near the eighth; as a generality, the old course was played in reverse with the clubhouse positioned above the current first green. The fifth and ninth were played over the A699 when roads were quieter places and a golf ball would be less likely to embed itself in the side of an Eddie Stobart awning.

After the *Briar Bank* first green, the course crosses the A699 and takes you downhill to *Caulk's Well* (spelt Caux's Well on the original layout) and the tee for *Pot Loch*. It is another blind uphill tee shot with severe dips and hollows scattered along its length. As you climb to the highest point of the fairway you are rewarded with fine views over the Linglie Hills and the distant rolling landscape of Ettrick and Yarrow. To the northeast are the Eildon hills, watching over Melrose. On any day this is a wild and wonderful place to play golf. The third takes you to the highest point on the course and the fourth takes you back; both have generous fairways which effectively join at the bottom of the hill and any slice from the fourth tee is likely to end up in the same place as your drive from the third.

My personal favourite is the fifth, *Pond*, a 384-yard downhill, par 4 right-hand dogleg. On both occasions I played this hole my drive held up to the right of the fairway leaving a long blind shot over trees to reach the green some thirty feet below. On both occasions I walked down the hill to find my ball securely on the green. A longer hitter would drive to the bottom of the hill and the green would open up before him, but where is the adventure in that. High handicappers have an entirely different narrative but we have our compensations.

The sixth is a short uphill par 3 where the top of the pin is only just visible; it is a very steep breathless climb to the summit after which you re-cross the A699 to the seventh. This is the only hole with a significantly different tee on the back 9, the sixteenth being 45 yards longer, which puts the green out of sight. From both there is a tendency for the ball to gather down to the right to some punishing rough.

The par 5 eighth is the club's signature hole, *Quarry*, a real test of golf particularly if you struggle to drive straight off the tee. The fairway is a long narrow avenue with sloping rough on both sides, the worst to the left. At 495 yards off the yellow tees you need to keep to the smooth surfaces if you are not going to be left with a long drive into the green for your third which, at almost any distance, is blind. Like the fifth there is a surprise to be had when you round the corner into the green, not always pleasant.

The final hole is named after Haining House, a Palladian mansion to the west of the course. Built and occupied by the Clan Pringle from the eighteenth century, the house and estate were bequeathed to the people of Selkirk in 2009 by an altruistic millionaire. At the time of writing, restoration of the mansion and establishment of a visitor centre is work in progress. In its neglected original state it is still possible to imagine that the shuttered blind windows mark the end of the season, the family trunks have been packed and loaded on the train heading south. All that remains are a few servants until everyone returns in the spring.

In September we caught the train for London with typewriter, dogs, bags and baggages and bicycles – David Thomson – *Nairn in Darkness and Light.*[2]

The house sits squarely in the landscape. In 1819, significant classical changes were commissioned by John Pringle: the Ionic loggia facing the loch and the arcaded portico to the north façade. However, something vital is missing. The six plinths across the terrace are empty of their Antonio Canova-inspired statues, removed to a safe place following vandalism in 2010; one was decapitated while another was pushed from its plinth. Pringle had kept a number of exotic animals on the estate including monkeys, a wolf and a bear and their cages remain. During the Second World War the house and estate were requisitioned by the military as a base for Polish troops who purportedly brought with them another bear, their famous mascot Corporal Wojtek (prn – Voy-Check); a star in his own right, he has even been the subject of a film, *The Bear That Went to War.*[3] Sadly, this story appears to be a convenient fiction, perhaps given credence by the con-tinuing existence of the cages – *The Bear that Wasn't*.[4] During the war, Wojtek saw active service at Monte Casino and became a true soldier, partial to both beer and cigarettes, eating rather than smok-ing; he did not arrive in Scotland with his Polish Regiment until 1946. His full remarkable story is immortalised in Aileen Orr's, *Wojtek The Bear, Polish War Hero* which confirms that he spent his last years of freedom at the Winfield Polish Resettlement Camp some forty miles to the east before being transferred to Edinburgh Zoo, his final home. Given the fate of the statues it is perhaps regrettable that the tradition of allowing wild animals onto the estate was not maintained, fictional or otherwise.

In its eccentricity, the estate bears some comparison with Ravello's Villa Cimbrone situated not far from Monte Casino where Wojtek saw action; it is also populated with Canova-inspired statues. In 1904 Cimbrone and its gardens were lovingly restored and enhanced by the 'Inglese', Ernest William Beckett, 2nd Lord Grimthorpe who must surely have known of the Haining. One glorious September afternoon we walked these gardens in the footsteps of long-departed house guests whispering of past lives and regrets: Greta Garbo, D. H. Lawrence, Vita Sackville-West, Edward James, Diana Mosley, Henry Moore, T. S. Eliot, Winston Churchill. From the Terrazza dell'infinito, *'the most beautiful view in the world'*, a clear blue sky merged as one with a bright blue sea at an indistinguishable horizon, we were at the absolute centre of the civilised world. Stage right from the terrace, a forest fire fanned by sea breezes created an apocalyptic vision as white smoke climbed the hillside, stretching towards Ravello. Later that after-noon in a back street café, news that the modern world had changed dramatically filtered through in half understood Italian. It was 11th September 2001. In the uneasy days and weeks that followed it felt like the enemy was at the door, but in truth, envious ignorant destruc-tion is ever present, even in the shadows of a Scottish border town.

Given the American right wing's obsession with firearms, what followed was surely no surprise. George W. Bush claimed he had given up golf out of respect for soldiers in Iraq. *'I don't want some mom whose son may have recently died to see the commander-in-chief playing golf,'* he said. *'I feel I owe it to the families to be in solidarity as best as I can with them. And I think playing golf during a war just sends the wrong signal.'* No such dilemma would have existed if the commander-in-chief and his ilk, the political wing of guns, gas and oil, had stuck to playing with balls rather than playing with soldiers.

*

Haining is a magnificent finish; a 151-yard par 3 from an elevated tee, some 45 feet above the green with fine views to the west. Can there be a more compelling, satisfying and rewarding sporting achievement than striking a golf ball from a high tee and watching it ride the air before its descent to the heart of the green. I think not; it is the delay between the action and the result, the sweet moments of expectation as the ball flies, hangs in the air and then begins its descent. Time stands still; the perfect ending to a near perfect course.

And so to Innerleithen which opens with a splendid par 3 also from an elevated tee but an altogether different proposition. The courses are approximately 17 miles and a half hour's driving apart and consequently ideally paired for a full day's golf in the wild. From the golf club entrance turn right down into the town, left into the high street and then follow the A707 and signs to Peebles, carrying straight on at Scott's courthouse and grey-painted monument rather than following the A7 to the right. Descending through the outskirts of the town, the A707 eventually crosses the Ettrick and turns right for Innerleithen and Peebles along Linglie Road. At Yair Bridge, a single-file turnpike bridge dating from the eighteenth century, the road crosses the Tweed which keeps close company with the A707 and the A72 for the rest of the journey. The A72 is joined beyond Caddonfoot passing through Walkerburn before reaching the outskirts of Innerleithen. On the south side of the Tweed there is much evidence of the single-track railway that opened between Edinburgh and Peebles on American Independence Day in 1855. This line was extended south to Galashiels by the *Innerleithen and Galashiels Railway* and opened in June 1866. The full length of the line from Eskbank through to Galashiels closed in February 1962 but much of the infrastructure remains in place and forms an integral part of the 18-hole golf course at Cardrona, 3 miles west of Innerleithen. The railway bridge over the Tweed links the east and west sections of the course while the station once acted as the clubhouse before the advent of the hotel complex.

As you come down the hill into Innerleithen, the road eases right over Leithen Water and the river bridge with its six ornate 'gas' lamps. Leithen Road, the route to the golf course, is an immediate sharp right after the bridge. A half mile up this road is Ronan's Well, an historic spa which also has connections with Sir Walter Scott, lending its name to his only novel set in the nineteenth century and peopled by such literary stalwarts as Dr Quakleben, Captain Hector MacTurk and the dastardly Sir Bingo Binks; surely all golfers to a man. One mile further north the valley opens out, the road turns right over Leithen Water by a narrow bridge, there is a tee box to your left and a green to your right. Suddenly you are in the heart of a golf course. Golf has been played in this valley for over 125 years, following the formation of the club at the Traquair Arms Hotel on 22nd September 1886. An invitation was sent to Willie Park senior of Musselburgh (Open Champion in 1860, 1863, 1866 and 1875), to lay out the course for the princely sum of ten shillings; by 1887 local golfers were competing for the first handicap medal. From the committee minutes of 1890 it is evident that the club competed in the *Border Challenge Shield* from the outset, the first match being scheduled at Hawick on 19th April followed by Innerleithen, Melrose, Kelso and finally Selkirk. The results of the challenge and the eventual permanent departure of the shield to Selkirk were not recorded.

The modern clubhouse rests on the site of the original wooden structure opened on 4th April 1896 with great pomp and ceremony by Sir Charles Clow Tennant, businessman, industrialist and Liberal politician. This building survived until 1942 when it mysteriously burned down at a time when the course had been abandoned during the Second World War. As a first step to reinstating the club in 1950, arrangements were made to acquire the clubhouse from the curling pond. I like to imagine this is the pint-sized green building with a corrugated roof that sits behind the current practice green and beneath the first tee. It actually bears some resemblance to the original clubhouse that appears in the Valentine 1912 postcard, a photograph taken from the high ground now occupied by the first tee. The view along the valley has changed little while the golfers' transport has changed utterly.

As introductions to golf courses go, this is almost unique. The tee is 15 feet above the clubhouse and some 30 feet higher than the distant par 3 green. To your right is the Leithen Road, behind the green is Leithen Water and along the entire route to the green there is a burn. It is an inspiring challenge; serious hackers will make use of the road camber. It is no wonder that the club emblem includes the words from Matthew 26:41: *Watch and pray*, which aptly continues, *that ye enter not into temptation: the spirit indeed is willing, but the flesh is weak.*

The second, a 343-yard par 4, runs parallel to Leithen Water and takes you to the most southerly end of the course where the green is protected by a tree and two bunkers to the left, which is only a concern if you stray onto the adjacent fairway. From here it is a steep climb to the third tee box, Pirn Craig, some 40 feet above the fairway where anything left will be reasonably safe and anything right is unlikely to be seen again. These three holes complete the trip *'round the loop'* and while this attractive section of the course looks like it has always been there, these holes were only added after the Second World War when land to the north of the course was reclaimed by a local farmer and three original holes lost. This was a recurring theme in the early days of the club, the agricultural fraternity resorting to ploughing and planting turnips on the fairways, driving stakes into the greens and littering the course with all sorts of farm machinery and rubbish; sometimes in ignorance, sometimes in malice.

Golf Course and Leithen Valley, Innerleithen

At the fourth the road comes back into play while a careless slice will take you back into the car park and an insurance claim. You are now playing into the original course layout, which appears in the 1912 postcard to the front of the clubhouse. Fortunately there doesn't seem to be a rush hour along Leithen Road, but there is sufficient movement on the road to demand some attention before driving off. An incident imprinted on my synapses: playing the eighteenth at Seahouses, my youngest son pulled his drive left into the windscreen of an oncoming Vauxhall Astra, fortunately not a group of Hells Angels. I was *livid*; I had hit a perfect drive down the middle and a par or even birdie looked a certainty; what might have been. By contrast, the dear lady driver who suffered the shock of her life, was remarkably understanding even as she picked glass from her hair. Ever since, I have been very wary of traffic.

This is not to suggest that the road through the course is somehow undesirable, far from it, this adds enormously to the unique character and flies gloriously in the face of the health and safety brigade. There are other clubs where a road dissects the fairways, but surely not one where it is such an integral part of the course. The glorious Machrie Bay on Arran has some similarities and their ninth is lethal; a 244-yard par 4 reachable in one by some, the green is within feet of the road. If you leave yourself with a long shot into the green, the consequences could be disastrous, not least because in the summer months this relatively fast road around the island can be very busy. No such dangers exist at Innerleithen where all traffic movement is clearly visible. Nor does Leithen Road detract from the wild nature of the course. This is an ancient road weaving its way across open empty moorland into the high hills, into a lost valley, the land that time forgot. This is a wild place.

Along the road is the fifth, *Hill* hole, a devious 100-yard par 3. In a sane world the tee and green would be reversed, but where would be the fun in that? Instead it is a pitch across the road to a blind green 30 feet above. The climb to the hole is done, as mountaineers would describe, in a traverse, assuming your ball is not lodged in the bank. If luck is with you, for luck it must be, *it will lay content, two paces from the pin.*[5]

The next is the first of two par 5s, this one squeezed between the ever-present road and a series of burns, one of which neatly idles by the front of the green. On my second visit I proudly avoided disaster and arrived in regulation only to be defeated by the tiered green; be warned. The seventh, *Lea Pool,* is a 180-yard par 3 taking you to the northern extremities of the course, running parallel to a practice area. Over the drystone wall, sheep graze where once there were tees, fairways and greens.

The next is the second par 5, a 524-yard stretch which runs parallel to the road and Leithen Water. The river runs close to your right so the temptation is to head left across the road. The local rules make no reference to this being out–of–bounds, although it does apply to the fifth/sixteenth. There is still a long way to go from either side of the road. The gap in the dyke marks the line to the hole which shares a double green with the fourth, a hole I three-putted out and back. The greens are excellent and true, so I cannot blame the greens staff nor the putter, just the incompetent attached to its northern end.

The fairways also run long and true and it is hard to imagine searching for a plugged ball on this turf. The 372-yard par 4, *Hame*, takes you back to the bridge and the clubhouse. It is a strong-willed golfer who can resist a second nine in this magnificent wild place.

In 1896 Leithen Water flooded the entire valley and deposited tons of sand on the course, the perfect foundation, and this will not have been the first time this happened over the millennia. Consequently, this inland course feels like links not moorland. When Open Champions Harry Vardon and Sandy Herd played here in 1905 they were moved to remark *'Better turf and greens plus the scenic appeal you could not wish for anywhere'*. It was true then, it is true now.

Notes

1.   The photograph of J. Jamieson, the club champion in 1893, is reproduced by kind permission of the Selkirk Golf Club and the Robert D. Clapperton Photographic Trust. The insert is the trophy as it appears today on the wall of the Selkirk clubhouse.

2.   When I first used this quote from David Thomson's McVitie Prize-winning memoir, I didn't appreciate that there was a distant family connection that emerges later in this book.

3. *Wojtek – The Bear That Went To War* – released in 2011, directed by Will Hood and Adam Lavis and narrated by Brian Blessed – inconveniently it makes no reference to the Haining, the bear seemingly having spent his entire time at Winfield Camp near Hutton in the Borders before being transferred to Edinburgh Zoo.

4. *The Bear That Wasn't* is a children's book by Frank Tashlin written in 1946.

5. From John Betjeman's classic poem about playing the course at St Enodoc – *Seaside Golf*.

To Fife

2

If this can happen to Jimmy, what chance do the rest of us have.
Chris Amon reflecting on the death of Jim Clark in 1968

Selkirk and Innerleithen are both members of the Borders Golfers' Association, so too is the club at Duns. As a young teenager I possessed a surprising amount of knowledge about this area which I would have been hard pushed to place on a map. I knew much about Chirnside, Edington Mains, Charterhall and the Border Reivers but nothing of the Scottish and English families that raided across the entire border country from the late thirteenth century to the beginnings of the seventeenth century. For me the Border Reivers had only one point of reference; Jim Clark in an Aston Martin DBR1.

Clark was my first and last real hero, and to this day his reputation and memory remain intact and untarnished. Purchase any copy of *Motor Sport* magazine and a glowing reference is certain to be found somewhere in its pages. For a generation of enthusiasts he represents a time, a place and the type of self-effacing reserved genius who is no longer allowed to exist in the age of the ever-present interviewer seeking a sound bite, however inane, however inarticulate.

The border country is synonymous with Clark, the quiet farmer from Edington Mains, the family home, along the road from Chirnside. His racing career started in the borders at Winfield Race Circuit and then Charterhall before moving on to conquer the world. Winfield Circuit was laid out on the site of the abandoned RAF Winfield Airfield adjacent to the Polish Resettlement Camp, and the home of 22nd Company Polish Army Service Corps (Artillery) and their active, enlisted mascot, Wojtek. Aileen Orr, writing in her book *Wojtek The Bear, Polish War Hero,* discovered that *'Many locals remember well the sight of*

*a soldier and a bear walking down the long straight road to Sunwick
– a stretch which was used by the late Formula One racing hero Jim
Clark, a local farmer and another local legend.'*

I saw him race but a few times and he did not disappoint. In a Lotus
Cortina he danced like a clown on the high wire making the rest look
ordinary. The picture from the 1966 Gold Cup at Oulton Park is
straight from *Boy's Own*. Clark, in a Lotus Cortina, had been in pursuit of a hugely more powerful American Ford Galaxie for most of the
race, losing touch on the straight, climbing into its boot through the
corners. With just a couple of laps remaining, the Galaxie ran out of
brakes coming into Old Hall, slammed into the sleepers and bounced
into the middle of the circuit. Clark can just be seen squeezing through
the wreckage before taking the chequered flag in front of an adoring
audience. Fifteen years old and your hero performs according to the
script, all my planets were in alignment.

His untimely death at Hockenheim, a miserable race in a joyless place, on 7th April 1968 rocked a racing world almost immune to such frequent tragic events. As an introspective teenager with a consuming passion for racing machines and their pilots, I was devastated. Angry at the injustice, disbelieving and deeply saddened – it was like your team was suddenly no more. Imagine if Manchester United had withdrawn from the football league after Munich. It felt deeply personal. For years motor racing was missing a vital ingredient.

I have found no direct connection between golf and Clark, but if he had an aversion it would be understandable. He attended public school at Musselburgh where the day began with a cold shower at 7am regardless of the season. This was followed by 'links', a 'ten minute jog' around old Musselburgh racecourse and the golf links which is encircled by the track. Not the kind of boyhood experience that develops a bond of affection for such places.

*

And so we head further north, away from the Border country and towards the light. The original aim was to avoid motorways, dual carriageways and major conurbations, but from Edinburgh to Glasgow a swathe of clutter stretches across the waistband of Britain and it is impossible to avoid. The solution is to use the motorways to get through it as quickly as your chosen vehicle, and the law, will allow.

Head back down the Leithen Road to the junction with the A72 and turn right, passing the Cardrona Golf and Country Club Hotel before reaching Peebles. Drive through the town centre continuing along the A72 where Neidpath Castle, perched on the northern bank of the Tweed, can be glimpsed through the trees on the left followed, a half mile later, by the equally solid Neidpath Viaduct built to carry the Symington to Peebles branch line over the Tweed. At Lyne Station a smaller but equally solid construction spans Lyne Water. Both have buttresses with inset crosses to ward off evil spirits. This is part of a catalogue of superstitions associated with bridges that stem from such structures being considered symbolic of the 'crossing over' from life to death. It was also believed that the devil would claim the soul of the first person to cross a newly constructed bridge such that an animal would be made to cross first. Many people will not cross a bridge behind a coffin or hearse while others believe that if you make a wish and then continue in silence, the wish will come true; the same is supposed to happen if you count to twelve or spit over the bridge railing. Bridge builders have been known to add wine, a coin or a bit of iron to the mortar used in placing the keystone to ensure the future good fortune of a bridge, but if this superstition was applied to the railway bridges, it was sadly ineffective against 'progress' and the omnipresent bottom line; so much endeavour cast aside.

Four miles on from Lyne, turn right onto the B7059 which follows Lyne Water to the junction with the A701 at the strangely named Romanno Bridge. Turn right, signposted Edinburgh and West Linton, and then one mile up the road rejoin the B7059, signposted West Linton, Historic Conservation Village. It is just over 2 miles to the junction with the A702 and the direct road to Edinburgh, 16 miles north. The road passes through Carlops, Silverburn and Easter Howgate before reaching the Edinburgh by-pass.

Here begins the only stretch of dual carriageway/motorway on this road trip. At Hillend fork left at the junction with the A703 and then descend onto the A720. After 5 miles turn left for the M8 and follow the signs for the Forth Road Bridge. Keep heading north along the A90 and then the M90, exiting at junction 5. At the top of the slip road turn right, signposted Glenrothes. Almost immediately turn left and then right following the signs for the *RSPB Nature Reserve and Gliding Centre*.

Heading along the B9097 the destination is visible on the horizon to the left – Bishop Hill. It is as steep as it looks. Turn left at the junction with the B9097 and then left again onto the B920, sign-posted Scotlandwell. The Bishop looms ever larger.

At Scotlandwell turn left onto the A911 and Bishopshire golf course is under a mile along this road, just south of Kinneswood. The golf club car park, clubhouse and war memorial are immediately adjacent to the road on the right. The small granite obelisk sits next to the clubhouse and commemorates the fallen of two world wars from the small Parish of Portmoak, twenty-one from the First and three from the RAF in the Second. The loss of so many souls from such a small parish in the 1914–1918 war must have devastated this small community and echoed down the decades that followed. A touching coincidence; among the fallen from the First World War is Ben Curtis who shares his name with the 2003 (British) Open winner, the first golfer since Francis Ouimet in the 1913 US Open to win a major championship on his debut.

Chapter

3

Bishopshire & Strathtay

When a lovely flame dies, smoke gets in your eyes. Jerome Kern and Otto Harbach[1]

I was raised in smoke, it is a wonder my lungs still function. Every room in my parents' 1930s semi had a fireplace and every one was used regularly. A Commer Karrier delivered huge chunks of black carbon that were dumped sack by sack into the coal cellar to the sound of distant thunder. Bucket by bucket the mountain was carried to each of the rooms until it was gone and the cycle started over. Fires were entertainment as well as warmth; jets of methane fizzed and popped, the coal cracked and turned from black to red to white, there were distant furnaces, caverns and caves in its heart; Dante's Inferno in miniature. Adding match heads in layers of silver foil provided more excitement. I have been playing with fire ever since. Outside the fogs came and stayed for weeks fed by all those home fires, steam engines and the heavy industry of Manchester's Trafford Park, a place of smells and smoke where Dad worked as an industrial chemist at ICI Dyestuffs Division; *Trapped Under the Smog of the Industrial Blanket.*[2]

I could navigate the Park's roads by smell; the warm wheat of Kellogg's, the hot electrical motors at Courtaulds, the melted rubber at the tyre recycling plant and the distinct but indecipherable odour from British Oxygen. ICI was a land of steam traps and huge 'sheds' where miraculously bright colours were born. The chemistry was sophisticated but the technology was not. The smells have gone, my father died in 2003 with lung complications, the roads have sprouted roundabouts and lost their familiarity; I can no longer find my bearings.

Dad was a twenty-a-day man; he started out on Woodbines *but soon hit the harder stuff.*[3] Un-tipped Senior Service, *The Perfection of Cigarette Luxury*, changed in the early 1960s to Kensitas, *Our Belief, The Finest Leaf.* Presented on the pack by an obese butler, Kensitas were smoked for the gift coupons and the much-thumbed catalogue. Then my sister started flying, a stewardess with British Eagle and later BOAC, whereupon my father sacrificed the free kitchenware for duty frees, mostly Rothmans. These came in 'crush-proof' boxes where the cigarettes were packed in offset rows of three. If you ran a safety razor in a line beneath the path of the pull tab it was possible to remove the top cellophane section and extract a cigarette. The cellophane could then be replaced intact and the pull tab still functioned; for years Dad was convinced that Rothmans' packing systems were unreliable but with so many 200 packs hoarded in the cupboard he never found the motivation to complain. I confessed years later and he was amused, mildly impressed by my teenage ingenuity.

I hated Senior Service but with great persistence grew into an addiction based on the illicit Rothmans, or to be truthful anything I could get. Later in life, I became adept at giving up, and after many false starts finally succeeded whereas Dad stuck with it beyond the point of return. His future is mapped out in this decisive moment. It is June 1943 on their honeymoon with the war two years from its end. Cigarette in mouth, Ken is obediently holding Peg's handbag and unknown to them, my sister is coming into life. In a moment of divine synchronicity, they have golf clubs in their hands.

I gave up smoking in my mid-thirties, so steep ascents generally don't leave me gasping. Bishopshire is an exception, not so much a golf challenge more a cardiac stress test. Opened on 11th April 1903, the 22-acre site was originally rented from a Mr Small for the grand sum of £5 each year and eventually purchased outright in 1923 for the princely sum of £470. This is an odd and imaginative place for a golf course, similar in length to Allendale, it adopts the same strategy for protecting itself, not so much laid out as carved into the hill side. By necessity the greens are mostly small and tucked away, chiselled into the landscape. The deep furrows running down Bishop and Munduff Hills reach into the golf course and determine the route of the par fours. The geography provides no other option, most of the par threes being squeezed in across the summit. To the tune of the *Grand Old Duke of York* they march you up the hill and they march you back down again – three times, six if you play the full eighteen and you should. If you don't, you miss out on the twelfth for this is actually a ten-hole course, not a nine. The views, the hills, the climb, everything conspires to leave you breathless.

The first, *Right o'Way,* starts as a mild ascent, which steepens as you approach the green, but even from a few yards out, the shape and size of the putting surface remains a mystery. Like many of the greens on the course it has banks on two sides, which once recognised can be used to some advantage. The greens are well kept and true, which is a major achievement as this course is entirely maintained by volunteers; there are no permanent employees. This is nothing short of miraculous, greenkeeping by committee decision and volunteer effort sounds almost unworkable. At Allendale we survive with one employed greenkeeper, working part time in the winter and one skilled, almost full time, volunteer. The only direction they receive is the occasional feedback from members through the committee and requests from the treasurer to rein in spending. This apart, they make all the decisions on course maintenance, equipment repair and associated purchases on their own. How this might be done through a collection of volunteers, however enthusiastic, I find difficult to imagine, but it evidently works well at Bishopshire, two of the committee members carrying out the task on a part-time basis. On the occasion I visited late in the year, the course was a credit to their endeavours. Enthusiasm, dedication and a love of the course is how many of these small nine-hole courses survive and their long-term chances are probably better than many of the larger undertakings where the administration overheads alone exceed the total turnover at Allendale and Bishopshire.

The second/eleventh climbs some more and confirms my view that you need not travel to Carnoustie to find golf holes that challenge. *Boyd's Best* is only stroke index 7/8, but it defeated me; Boyd must be the local sadist. No doubt locals will wonder what the fuss is about, but this is just the sort of hole where I struggle. At only 138 straight yards it should be simple but it is not. The approach is steep and gets steeper as you approach the green such that anything short will stop dead; by contrast, unless you can throw the ball very high over this sort of distance, then anything long is going to be through the green and into trouble. Well done Boyd, whoever you are.

This is more or less the summit and the third, *Hog's Back*, plays across the hill to a small green beyond a burn, just 92 yards away. The twelfth, *Waterdoon '92*, slightly further up the hill, plays to an adjacent green over a distance of 109 yards. It was at this point on the front nine that I became aware that I was being watched. Circling silently above me like a flock of predatory pterosaurs were seven gliders in alarmingly close company, riding the thermals above Munduff and Bishop Hills. As they circled they would disappear behind the hill, forage for heaven knows what and then, reappear a few moments later, sated. I am sure it is a satisfying pastime, but I prefer to be more solidly attached to Earth.

A good friend who combines a passion for flying with a far too generous 23 handicap tells a salutary tale. On the last day of a week-long course he was gliding at several thousand feet above the Yorkshire countryside when his instructor calmly and without explanation requested that he take over the controls. They descended gently and landed without drama. My friend, a true Yorkshireman who demands his money's worth, was disgruntled that he had been deprived of his last landing opportunity and so approached his instructor who sat head in hands and occasionally taking deep lung-filling drags on a cigarette. When questioned, the instructor remained silent but opened the palm of his hand; there lay a collection of split pins used to hold the wing securing bolts in place – without them, the bolts are free to pop out in turbulence and the wings drop off. They had been in his pocket throughout the flight; my friend, a non-smoker, sat down next to him and demanded to share his cigarette. I will stick to golf.

There are challenges enough on a golf course and the fourth/thirteenth at Bishopshire, *Loch View*, provides ample evidence. Climbing to an elevated tee you are presented with a magnificent panorama: the Loch Leven nature reserve, its islands and in the distance the Ochil Hills. The shallow depression that is filled by Loch Leven was formed by glacial movement in the last Ice Age. Meltwaters from the retreating glaciers partly filled the loch with sand and gravel such that half is less than two metres deep, the shallow water and secluded shoreline providing an ideal home for ducks, swans and shore-side plants. More than 35,000 waterfowl visit the Loch in autumn and on the day I played Bishopshire vast numbers took to the air, the height of the course is such that you are on a level with their flight path. The gliders circling above, the massed birds in skeins above the Loch and the far-reaching views add to the sense of playing golf across the sky.

When the clouds settle on Munduff Hill and fogs creep down the ravines, this must be an altogether different and eerie place. The views will disappear and no longer will you see back to the Forth Rail Bridge and less inspiringly, the flame from the ethylene plant near

Cowdenbeath. Ethylene copolymers are used for many things, not least the manufacture of modern golf balls – all in a good cause then.

The secondary panorama is the fourth fairway and it is daunting. Straight ahead there is uncompromising rough riding the back of the ridge that reaches down from the hill. Slightly to the right is the fairway in the dip and then another ridge with a burn hugging its shoulder. There is precious little room for error, no room to go left and anything drifting right is likely to be lost. I sacrificed two balls to the golfing gods on this hole alone and received very little by way of thanks. Once clear of the ridges the approach to the green is straightforward, as long as you don't pitch too long onto the A911.

The fifth/fourteenth, *Sheltered Valley*, a 240-yard par 4, takes you back up the hill while up on the left is the elevated sixth/fifteenth tee box, a 161-yard par 3, Kilmagad Wood. The green sits in front of the seventh tee box and is completely blind. Anything right will find the seventh fairway whereas anything left will find trouble, possibly poor innocents on the seventh tee. It is another challenging hole best played with a look-out.

With this in mind it is possibly best not to linger at the seventh/sixteenth tee even though the views are arresting. Running across the top of the course and the back of the seventh tee is the Michael Bruce Way, a footpath which circumnavigates Kinneswood, Scotlandwell and Portmoak Moss. Several other paths, one starting to the left of the clubhouse, take you to the top of Bishop and Munduff Hills and into the Lomond Hill Regional Park, while to the south of the main road another follows the shore of Loch Leven. Even without a set of irons this is serious walking country. The poet and hymnist, Michael Bruce, 1746–1767, was born in Kinneswood; a contemporary of Burns he is known as *the gentle poet of Loch Leven* and is buried in the parish churchyard. It was his childhood in this landscape that inspired his best work, and standing on the seventh tee the source of his inspiration is there for all to see. On this bright autumn day, the bracken had turned a winter rust, far away geese rose from Loch Leven and the islands floated on a thin layer of silver. It is indeed an inspirational place.

The seventh/sixteenth 348-yard par 4, *Wood March*, runs back down the hill and is much less daunting than the fourth. There is trouble left, but anything leaking right is probably destined for the 5th fairway, assuming the ball does not snag in the trees. And then it is back up the hill again, although only about half way.

The eighth/seventeenth, *Burnside*, is beyond the fifth tee box and fourth green, and then it comes as something of a surprise that you are actually playing the fourth in the opposite direction, although the course guide imaginatively suggests more acreage than is actually available. This is no criticism, quite the opposite, in an age obsessed with health and safety this is a creative use of limited space, but I imagine a busy competition day could be 'interesting'. The green is tucked into the side of the left-hand ridge, the green I flirted with from the fourth tee. Like almost all approaches on this course, your pitch to the eighth green must be pinpoint accurate.

The last is *Castle Island*, a 193-yard par 3 (281-yard par 4 from the whites) back to the clubhouse with the same burn that troubled the eighth offering the same obstacle on this final hole. Castle Island, after which the hole is named, floats on Loch Leven and is the place where Mary Queen of Scots was imprisoned from 17th June 1567 until her escape on 2nd May 1568. This would have been a significant news event which today would demand wall-to-wall coverage on Sky News and BBC News 24, a host of outside broadcast vehicles, miles of cabling, a sea of satellite dishes and hours of speculation; nothing like it had happened before in this small parish and probably nothing has happened since. Mary had a keen eye for life's priorities as she reputedly played Musselburgh Old Links not long before her imprisonment in the same year, 1567; she was also expecting twins. At the moment of her beheading twenty years later at Fotheringay Castle, her last thoughts were also about a swing. Unfortunately for Mary, the executioner was a high-handicap hacker who took three from the tee, part of an unnecessarily sadistic ritual designed to extend the suffering of the victim, decapitation not being sufficient punishment. That or it was just plain incompetence dressed up as something else. Bishopshire did not open until 1903 and the first clubhouse not until 1912, so there were no final rounds for Mary, and this is a pity for the course deserves greater renown.

And so to Strathtay. The route completes a round trip of Loch Leven, turning right from the course and heading north through Kinneswood, Balgedie and Milnathort, approximately 5 miles back to the M90. This stretch of motorway is the last on the road trip and has some memorable stretches, particularly the descent towards Perth passing Bridge of Earn and overlooked by Moncrieffe Hill. At the M90/A9 junction follow the signs for Inverness skirting Perth to the south and west; stay on the A9 for another 14 miles north from the Inveralmond roundabout and then watch for the B898, turning to the left signposted Dalguise. This marks the end of dual carriageways and motorways, from here on it is driving as it used to be. This sleepy road runs parallel with the A9 to the west of the Tay and is a much more attractive if slower alternative passing through Dalmarnock, the Kinnaird Estate and Balnaguard before emerging at the junction with the A827, a mile east of Strathtay. In the centre of Grandtully turn right across the single-track bridge over the Tay, signposted Strathtay Golf Course, a quarter of a mile. Over the bridge carry straight on by the war memorial and at the top of the hill turn right. The golf course is now on your left; follow the road for 325 yards to the entrance of the small car park.

The clubhouse and honesty box are across the first and tenth fairways, and from the moment you arrive it is obvious that this is a wonderful place to play golf. While there is immediate evidence of two fairways and greens running parallel to the road, it is also apparent that behind the clubhouse and woods there is steep rising ground and the immediate question is, where on earth is the rest of the course?

The golf club was established in 1909 by Captain John Malcolm Steuart of Ballechin, owner of the Tullypourie Estate, forfeiting prime grazing land in the pursuit of his passion. The Captain took the lead in establishing the course, his wife striking the first ball just six weeks after the layout was started. A picture of the clubhouse on its opening day, with forty or so members posing for the camera, shows a building little changed over 100 years later. It is now protected from errant golf balls by a tall wire fence and fronted by a small terrace, otherwise it is much the same. On the fine autumn day I played there was not another soul to be seen, and only when I reluctantly drove away some four hours later did I see an ageing gentleman practising his putting on the second green, his dog watching patiently. Much like Allendale, this dedicated access to a wonderful course is great for the golfer but not so good for the club's coffers, and yet, these small clubs continue to survive even through the harshest economic times. Their greatest enemy is the weather. Most are situated in a small catchment area such that membership numbers can be relatively small. Thus green fees represent a larger than normal proportion of annual income and a wet summer can do serious damage to the bottom line. However, unencumbered by large loans, very few if any salaried employees and a small but loyal band of members, their prospects are healthier than many 'stay and play' hotels or golf complexes boasting floodlit driving ranges and 7,000-yard marathons for golfers whose main ambition is to strike the ball the furthest possible distance from the tee, into the nearest artificial lake. There is nothing artificial about Strathtay, you simply play the ground as God intended; this is not the product of massed JCBs. Depressingly, the 'experts' now tell us that we are in the middle of a 10–20 year cycle of wet summers, information which they should have kept to themselves bearing in mind it serves no useful purpose and is probably nonsense.[4]

To celebrate their centenary in 2009, the club enhanced the course by an imaginative addition of nine tee boxes, such that the back nine can offer an altogether different approach to the same hole.

The first par 4 and the second par 3 are a relatively gentle introduction, played across what must be some of the flattest land in the district, the perfect size for a football pitch. Indeed, the club's history reveals that this hallowed ground has been shared with Grandtully Vale football team, grazing sheep and battle-hardened warriors. Beneath the tenth tee a stone coffin was discovered containing an armoured skeleton suggesting that more than just football and golf matches have been contested across this land.

It is at the third that the course begins to reveal its true nature. The green nestles between two copses and on the front nine is approached from a tee box some sixty feet above; the climb is as steep as you can make without requiring crampons, but on arrival the views are breath-taking.

The green is plain to see, although the flight of the ball into a low autumn sun can be a mystery; if you worry about hitting the ball straight, a 'fade' to the copse to the right is less punishing than a 'draw' to the left. On the back nine the same green is approached on the level over tall and ancient beech trees; 'fade' or 'draw' makes no difference, the real test is to lift the ball high enough to clear the trees and yet still have the length to reach the green over 170 yards distant. From either tee it is a real test of golf but less a test of your respiratory system on the way back.

Similarly, the fourth offers radically different approaches on the front and back; on the way out the tee is set at ground level and the par 3 green, *Marsh*, is 133 yards distant on a narrow elevated ridge – a steep bank to the front, stone wall and copse to the right, there is no easy hiding place. On the back nine, the thirteenth, *Lagans*, plays to the same green, but this time you have to climb the sixty feet to a tee adjacent to the third; the green lies beneath you to the right. It is like landing the ball on an upturned dinner plate. Remarkably, I put the ball plumb-centre at first attempt and now I have no desire to play the hole again, secure in the knowledge I could never repeat the trick. I occasionally have this problem with entire courses, played well at first attempt, I am reluctant to return and taint the memory. My shrinking world excludes Alnmouth Village (7 pars out of 9), Consett (sixteen

stableford points after 5 holes), Wooler (seventeen stableford points after 6 holes), Musselburgh Old Course (drove straight and long all day and hardly missed a putt) and Seahouses (for reasons mentioned earlier). Life can be the same; places and people best remembered for their better days.

The fifth, 203-yard par 4 is unique; *Spion Kop* is a serious challenge. Played back up the hill from inside the copse, what faces you from the tee appears to be a near vertical grass bank with a marker post at its summit. The name reflects the terraced nature of the hill and pays homage to Captain Steuart's first-hand experience of the Boer War and the infamous defeat of the British at this strategic hill near Ladysmith, South Africa in 1900. The name has been used at sporting venues since the early twentieth century, the first recorded reference relating to Arsenal's Manor Ground in 1904 when a local reporter likened the silhouette of fans standing on a newly raised earth bank to *soldiers standing atop the hill at the Battle of Spion Kop*. It is ironic that in a sport where defeat cannot be countenanced, the Kop is synonymous with the Anfield mass demanding victory at any cost. Bill Shankley's much celebrated but entirely flawed quote, *'Football isn't a matter of life or death, it's much more important than that'*, could be qualified with *'second only to a rounded education'*.

I am sure some could drive the top of the hill, but my ball had reached its zenith long before the top of the bank, dropped, briefly settled and then rolled back some six feet before nestling in a tuft of grass; how the greenkeeper might cut this bank is a mystery. The next challenge is to climb the hill, with as few clubs as necessary, find the ball and adopt a seriously contorted stance in order to pitch the ball over the ridge. At this stage what might lay beyond remains a mystery to the newcomer and it would be no surprise to find a Boer encampment as you crest the rise. Instead there is narrow green in a hollow approached by steps and with luck your ball sitting in bright contrast on the green. If not, then it could be anywhere in the rough that surrounds the hole; a mighty hitter is likely to find serious trouble if he attempts to drive this green in one. As with many of these courses, the landscape provides more than enough protection to the greens without the introduction of man-made contrivances.

Hopefully among the clubs dragged to the top of the hill you will have remembered a driver, for the sixth provides an opportunity to let rip from a great height. This hole, the only one over 300 yards, weaves its path along the back of the copse behind the clubhouse and emerges next to a conveniently located cottage after which it is named. I don't know the acreage of the course, but it must be small even relative to other nine-holers and yet, for the most part, you are not crossing fairways nor would you be putting life and limb at risk if the course were busy, it is just a well-crafted use of space. If you can drive long and straight then going left over the hillock will find the fairway as it doglegs towards the cottage and green; anything heading right is liable to find the copse; there must be a fine store of balls in those woods, two of them belong to me. The seventh is a relatively short par 3 approached from two tee boxes adjacent to the cottage and is straightforward if you hit the green, anywhere else and all bets are off.

And then there is the eighth, *Gushat*. This is the name of the building in Grandtully that was once occupied by a foundry and now the village shop; at first I had assumed it was an ancient Gaelic expletive. On the back nine the same hole from a slightly different tee is called *Hope* – the sign writer presumably ran out of space for *'Abandon all'*. This hole is a devilish rascal. To the left are tall trees and out-of-bounds and to the right is the cottage, the gap between seems mighty narrow. Right, beyond the cottage is heavy, ball-consuming rough, so straight and long it must be – I managed it on the way out, but knew I could not repeat the trick on the way in – another ball gone. I saw no occupants in the cottage and while there is fencing to offer some protection, landing a ball in the front garden is certainly not beyond the bounds of possibility. The residents are either keen golfers or remarkably tolerant. Hence the last comes as a relief, a short par 3 where the only danger is bunkers – the last ball in your pack of six should be safe.

I left Strathtay with some reluctance as it is a fine and unlikely piece of ground for a golf course which demands consistently good shot-making to conquer. With ten par 3s and eight par 4s it is only 3,601 yards off the yellow tees, nearly *two miles* shorter than the bigger 18-hole tracts. This merely serves to emphasise that distance is an irrelevant ingredient for enjoying a round of golf. I must and I will return; I have a fine collection of golf balls to retrieve from the woods.

Notes

1. The song *Smoke Gets in Your Eyes* was originally written for the musical *Roberta* in 1933. The most famous recording is probably by The Platters in 1958. I first remember it from the reworded Esso Blue paraffin adverts which ran from the 1950s to the early 1970s.

2. The title *Trapped Under the Smog of the Industrial Blanket* is a track by the northern post-punk Indie band *A New Breed of Monkey* who *must* be far too young to remember such things.

3. The full lyric *I started out on Burgundy but soon hit the harder stuff*, from Bob Dylan's *Just Like Tom Thumb's Blues* first recorded in 1965 and released on the *Highway 61 Revisited* album.

4. Written in 2012, the dry summer of 2013 only helped confirm my suspicions.

To Killin

It was the best of times, it was the worst of times.
A Tale of Two Cities – Charles Dickens

Strathtay seems a solid and dependable place. Large Victorian houses once stood proud upon the village hillsides, but with time they have come to hide behind the maturing trees and tall hedgerows, perhaps embarrassed by their outward signs of prosperity. It was the arrival of the railway at Grandtully, on the opposite bank of the Tay, which attracted the well-heeled, putting Dundee, Perth, Edinburgh and Glasgow within commuting distance. The line closed in 1965, exactly 100 years after it opened, and nearly another fifty years on I am sure it is still missed; a line which stretched into the upper reaches of the Tay and Aberfeldy would have been a magnificent journey.

Strathtay and Grandtully remind me of the towns where I was brought up, the prosperous southern suburbs of Manchester: Altrincham, Bowdon and Hale which also grew from the arrival of the railways. We were not prosperous, but there were certainly plenty who were, holed up in grand mansions on the rising ground above Altrincham. However, you didn't need to live in some grand pile to attract life's conveniences and luxuries, even modest dwellings were built with the expectation of live-in staff. My good friend William, his Mum and Dad, Sylvia and Douglas, lived in a fairly modest semi just outside Hale, but above the kitchen door there was a panel with indicators for every room in the house and in each room a push-button Bakelite switch to summon the servant, not that there were any by then.

This was my second home and a convenient bolt-hole for when I was in disgrace, a more than regular occurrence. There was always a fire burning in the 'snug', a cosy back room which included a vast classical and jazz record collection, a small lathe where Douglas could recreate Lotus racing cars in miniature, Sylvia's hat-making tools and a squashy sofa for lounging about on or fighting with just William. On the walls hung several oil paintings by Douglas, all nudes, for this was his career, a lecturer in life drawing at Manchester University. Sylvia always claimed he had the best job in the world, and it was certainly a career that both William and I aspired to, even though neither of us could draw a curtain. The kitchen-diner had a vast self-centred Aga which required constant attention and an oval pine table where we sat for meals and entered into real conversation. There was much talk about the motor racing news of the day, occasionally art and architecture. Sylvia could entertain with whole passages from P G Wodehouse, she seemed entirely consumed by Blandings Castle. To the front of the house was her 'museum', a dark plush dining room, each wall given over to display cases for her collection of antique jewellery. I was always happy there and in typical teenage 'Kevin and Perry' style, I was always on my best behaviour.

I left them all behind but William, after a series of failed relationships, stayed for the duration. Sylvia died young as did William, such that Douglas, left alone with the ghosts of Lord Emsworth and the Empress of Blandings, soon followed his only son. It is odd to think of that house without them and I do not wish to see it.

Because William lived 'down the road' from me, it was always from here that adventures began. Each season in the 1960s there were at least three non-championship Formula 1 races in the UK, sometimes more, so the sight and sound of Grand Prix cars was not a once-a-year event. The Race of Champions, the International Trophy and the Gold Cup were virtually guaranteed entries from all the UK-based teams and they were the majority. Ferrari might not always show, but when the red transporter did arrive in the paddock it seemed like the event had been blessed by the Pope; it was to be a serious motor race. Consequently, without ever attending a Grand Prix I had seen plenty of Formula 1 cars in action, mostly at the end-of-season Oulton Park Gold Cup. For the first time, in 1968, I attended a Grand Prix proper at Brands Hatch. For three days in a warm July I was immersed in a glamorous but still accessible world. The race was held on a Saturday with practice days on the Thursday and Friday, and while there was a large attendance on race day, the practice days were relatively quiet, perhaps because your average working man was doing just that. A set of slides from those long-ago practice days show sparsely populated grandstands and unfettered access to the cars and drivers in the paddock. The entrance fee for race day was twenty shillings while access to the paddock on practice days was free. The cars were delivered in transporters that for the most part were badly converted coaches with cars being worked on in the open on a sloping paddock and not so much as an awning; everything and everybody was accessible to a pair of inquisitive schoolboys.

The 1968 Formula 1 cars were all hardware. The only on-board software came in the form of the largely unprotected driver. The face of the moon that rose over Brands Hatch on Friday 19th July remained unconquered, but NASA was about to change all that. A reasonably sized computer mainframe in 1968 probably came with 32K core memory, some 8 megabyte exchangeable disc drives, a card reader, paper tape reader, rows of magnetic tape drives and an air-conditioned room the size of a large family bungalow. By the end of the century a Formula 1 Grand Prix car would be exploiting unimagined increases in computing power and carrying a substantial proportion around the track. The late Christopher Evans produced some thought-provoking comparisons in his 1979 book, *The Mighty Micro*. If in 1945 you had wanted to build a computer containing the same number of functional elements as the human brain the machine would have been the size of Greater London. With the advent of transistors this had shrunk to the size of the Albert Hall and at the time of the 1968 British Grand Prix, the first integrated circuits would have reduced the machine to the size of a London bus. The seeds of computer miniaturisation sown by the space race changed the world forever. As Evans so rightly foresaw, *'very small computers have enormous advantages: firstly because they consume minute amounts of power; secondly, because they are very cheap; and thirdly, because they are extremely portable and can therefore be put to use in all kinds of different places'*. They cover a modern Grand Prix car like a rash.

As I turn right out of the entrance to Strathtay Golf Club towards Aberfeldy along the north side of the River Tay, I am cocooned in a car which contains more computing power than was launched into space during the entire Apollo programme. I am guided by a bunch of orbiting satellites which communicate with a computer that sits in the palm of my hand. My entire record collection, in excess of 8,000 tracks, is stored and played on an even smaller hand-held device which relays the sound through the car's stereo system. To cap it all, this same little machine can make a telephone call to anywhere in the world without the need for wires. My seventeen-year-old self would have considered all this ludicrous science fiction.

There was no pit lane telemetry in 1968, so the regular mechanical failures came out of the blue. The entry list for that year included four Coopers and four BRMs out of a field of just twenty-one starters. Cooper was in terminal decline while BRM would have a brief resurgence before also being consigned to the history books. The Owen Organisation entered three works BRMs for Rodriguez, Attwood and Lanfranchi – none finished. After two hundred and twelve miles, just eight cars were circulating at the chequered flag, the list of retirements including both works Gold Leaf Team Lotus cars; Graham Hill retiring after twenty six laps with a broken half shaft and Jackie Oliver just after half-distance with transmission problems.

The year was a turning point for Grand Prix racing. The sponsorship of Gold Leaf Team Lotus was the first example of a tide of commercialism that would eventually engulf all forms of motor sport. The additional money funded research and development of cars beyond the afford-ability of the amateur. This year and this race specifically marked the ninth and final Grand Prix win for the Johnnie Walker whiskey heir, Rob Walker, the last of the true privateers. The car he entered was a Lotus 49 recently purchased from Colin Chapman, painted in the blue and white-striped Scottish racing colours and trusted to the hands of Jo Siffert who brought the car home in first place.

Ghosts follow us everywhere. Prior to his death in April, Jim Clark had won the South African Grand Prix at Kyalami on New Year's Day. Consequently, his name appears in the 1968 Championship table for the last time as a result of this, his last GP win. After South Africa, Gold Leaf Team Lotus headed 'down under' for the Tasman series, an event for GP cars but restricted to 2.5 litres. The 'downgraded' Lotus was identified as the 49T and was used by Clark to win the series, which comprised four races in New Zealand and four races in Australia. On its return to the UK the 49T was rebuilt to GP specification and sold to Rob Walker in time for the British GP, replacing an earlier version destroyed in a workshop fire. Thus, the photograph of the Rob Walker Lotus, taken from the upper level of the old Brands Hatch two-tier paddock, is of Clark's last Lotus 49.

*

It is quicker to head back across the bridge to Grandtully and right along the A827, but turning right out of the golf club and heading along the single-track road signposted Cluny Gardens is a much more rewarding if slower experience, because you are brought into close proximity with the river along much of its length and are forced to follow the slow contours of the landscape.

The road emerges to the northwest of Aberfeldy and it is here that it is probably wise to return to the wider roads. Turn left along Poplar Avenue sign-posted Aberfeldy a half mile. The road continues along the flat with the town golf course on the left crossing the Tay at William Adam's humped-back bridge, complete with ornate parapets and four obelisks pointing like Saturn rockets at the sky. Once over the bridge turn immediately right, passing the Black Watch monument before arriving at the junction with the A827. Turn right again and head due west with the Tay now on your right. It is 6 miles before Kenmore where the road crosses the Tay again and heads along the north side of Loch Tay. For most of its 16-mile length the A827 offers high panoramic views of the Loch before descending towards Killin. The entrance to Killin Golf Club is on your left and, on the occasions I have visited, it was helpfully highlighted by strings of bunting. If you pass the Bridge of Lochay Hotel you have missed the entrance, just.

4 Killin

The man who can smile when things go wrong has thought of someone else to blame.
Robert Bloch

This book exists because of Killin. It was here in 2005 that the idea of solitary golf in wild places was first born. Staying at the southern end of Loch Lomond and keen to escape a shopping expedition to Glasgow, I headed north along the A82 through Luss, Tarbet, Ardlui, Crianlarich and then east along Loch Glen Dochart to find the peace and solitude of Killin. On that glorious May day, heading down the par 5 eighteenth after a happy round to par, it occurred to me that I cannot be alone in my desire for solitary golf in the wild. There must be others for whom almost anything, but especially golf, is the perfect alternative to the dreaded retail therapy.

Killin Golf course sits on the edge of the fast-flowing River Lochay, which a further mile downstream meets the Dochart before both spill into Loch Tay. It is overlooked to the west by Sròn a Chlachain and Creag Bhuidhe, the Tarnamachan Ridge and Ben Lawers to the north with far-reaching views to Beinn Leabhainn and the mountains that rise from Glen Dochart to the south and west; the golf course is embraced by river and mountain. It is a wild and beautiful landscape and there is a sense of being on the edge of something more untamed than the eastern end of Loch Tay; this feels like the beginnings of the real high lands. The finest view of Killin, the golf course and all the way east along Loch Tay is to be found at the summit of Sròn a Chlachain. It is an arduous steep climb to 1,700 feet from Breadalbane Park in the centre of Killin, but it is worth the effort. On a clear day the Killin greens will glow on the valley floor, those smooth, manicured surfaces, too often the scene of my downfall.

*

I blame my parents for many things, not least my inability to putt. I was raised in a cul-de-sac. Alstead Avenue was home to twenty semi-detached houses built in the 1930s. A footpath circumnavigated the avenue and between the gates of each semi-detached pair there was a strip of grass with a privet bush at its centre. At the top of the street there was a gas lamp, which in the 1950s was still lit manually each night with the aid of two horizontal bars either side for the lamplighter to rest his ladder. They were ideally suited for young children to swing from, monkey-like. It was a safe haven with few cars and plenty of space, especially when you included the various front and back gardens, endless hiding places, garden sheds, garages and even purpose-built holes in the ground. There was a group of nearly a dozen children, all of a similar age who one autumn must have gone indoors as the days shortened never to return in the spring. That unnamed winter they had grown too old to run in and out of the houses, but I don't remember when; it was the moment when the carefree child turned into the uncertain, rebellious teenager.

How much self-belief, how much confidence do we need in life? In these modern materialistic times, children can be instilled with too much, such that the future has all the ingredients for disappointment. Provide them with too little and their true potential might never be realised. If you were raised in the 1950s the balance definitely swung in favour of 'be seen and not heard' – what the neighbours thought was paramount. *You taught me not to go overboard, lose my head, or make a big deal out of it, but to keep a happy medium, that the truth is in the middle. No extremes. Don't exaggerate. Hold your horses. Keep a lid on it. Save it for later. Be careful. Weigh the alternatives. Wear navy blue* - Garrison Keillor.[1] Growing up, 'maturing', is about trying to find the right balance and not all succeed.

For me, there was more to it than this. Old women in particular were frightening creatures. My small world was populated with the patch-work remains and disappointments from two world wars. There was the old lady in the brown mac with matching beret who talked to her-self incessantly. Head down, she walked twenty or so paces, turned around, looked up and walked three paces backwards, eyes peeled for something only she could name. She then turned around and started all over again. I never saw her do anything else. Always the same, locked into a world only she could see. I would cross the road to avoid her, desperate that our eyes should not meet. She haunted my dreams. There was the frail old lady up the street who had the face of a man and screamed at the neighbours who had stolen her rations, long after rationing ended. There were all the other ladies, who according to Peg, sat in judgement on my every action. I was perpetually watched, or so I was told.

And then there was Mum herself who had a penchant for the dramatic. Her two favourite outbursts were *'You will put me in Macclesfield Asy-lum!'* or, on more extreme days, *'Keep on like that and I will put my head in the oven!'* Before I understood the asphyxiating properties

71

of coal gas, I was fascinated by this prospect. How would this work exactly, how practical was it to bake your head, how effective would this be with the oven door open?

I remember this very clearly. I was pre-school and certainly of an age when moderately tall grown-ups towered like giants. Outside Woolworths in George Street, Altrincham, Mum was in conversation with an elderly neighbour, *'I am not going through that again, he is definitely the last. If it happens again you will find me in Macclesfield Asylum!'* The meaning was lost on me, but the memory of the words was not and this dark place called Macclesfield became another entry in my catalogue of fears. In reality, Macclesfield is a fine place famed for its silk industry; Macclesfield Parkside Hospital, a County Lunatic Asylum built between 1868 and 1871, was not. Closed in 1966, it is now a housing estate and I wonder if the residents realise that they sleep among the endless corridors of so many sad souls; despite her many threats Mum was never destined to join them.

There is a picture of me walking our urban street beside my mother. I am dressed too smartly in school uniform under a duffel coat, shorts and school cap. She looks imperious; she has seen Dad taking a photo from my sister's bedroom window and *we are not amused*. It is the headscarf that does it; it is royalty on their day off and there I am, the reluctant heir to the throne, too smartly dressed, head down, lost, unsure of everything. This is not the way I wanted to be and this is not the way Peg was. In private she would break wind at random and swear like a trooper. She had a fiery temper which at its peak would turn physical – plates, even chairs, became airborne. A swift sharp slap was de rigueur, painful at ten, just tedious at seventeen. Prolonged weekend arguments when bitter unforgivable words were exchanged with my father were my childhood dread. All of this conducted at high volume; *what must the neighbours have thought.*

The eternal theme – what other people think. It can take a lifetime to put behind you; now, with some outside assistance, I don't care, I don't give a monkey's. Except, standing over a short putt I am not thinking what is the line, what is the pace, I am thinking what will *they* say when I miss; I can hear them thinking *why is he taking so long!* So nothing has changed after all, reduced to my childhood self by a small white ball that might not drop in the hole even at the second attempt. Golf is a window on the soul.

*

In the twenty-first century we are more sophisticated and care little what the neighbours might think, this because for the most part we barely know who they are. We commute, we travel for leisure, we drive to the shops, constantly on the move, our friends are distant and we are thus no longer obliged to get on with those who live on our doorstep. However, there is a downside. In a crisis, taken unwell, no longer mobile, we become isolated and alone, there is no safety net. Ironically, the more isolated the community the less likely this is to happen, the old social norms remain intact. In small out-of-the-way villages where travel for social events is not practical, people make their own entertainment and in so doing interact, make friends and come to depend upon each other. Allendale is a fine example, and in 2007 won the *Calor Gas Village of the Year* award which *recognises vibrant, self-sustaining village communities which, irrespective of size, have made the best of local opportunities to maintain and enhance the quality of life for all residents.*

In plain English, it is a good place to live. The basic ingredients for a thriving community seem to be, in no particular order: a school to keep children close to home; a library and village hall as centres for gathering; pubs, cafés, some small shops, at least one being a local butcher and finally a catchment area too small to warrant the attentions of the larger supermarket chains but sufficient to justify a local Co-op.

This is the common ground between Killin and Allendale and of course, both have thriving local golf clubs which far from representing an elitist sport for the well-heeled and ungifted, play a major part in the sense of local community. As we travel north to further and further isolated villages the more important the golf club becomes and the more important the opinions of our neighbours; this is no bad thing. At the beginnings of the twentieth century, when many of these golf courses were formed, the other essential ingredient was access from public transport, which at that time meant one thing, the railways.

Killin seems an unlikely location for a railway and walking the village there is little immediate evidence that it ever existed, but if you amble over the bridge at Dochart Falls and turn immediately left at the Inn, some 400 yards down the lane on the left you pick up the path that takes you over the impressive Dochart Railway Viaduct. The line descends gently to the lower end of the village where the name *Station Road* identifies its original location but little else.

The photograph[2] from August 1950 shows a small station providing an essential service to the local community; a well-populated platform, some passengers (not customers) with suitcases and the ubiquitous milk churns, reminiscent of the picture of golfers on the platform at Allendale.

This was more than a means of transport. It was a physical representation of a connection between outlying communities and the rest of the world. The rails converging to infinity speak of the romance of travel to faraway places and a safe return home. If the grand city stations were the cathedrals then the small country versions were the wayside shrines, worshipping the gods of arrival and departure. The joy of a loved one's return overcame public inhibition as we embraced their safe arrival amid the clatter of the engine at rest, half hidden in the swirling steam. The departure was prolonged, determined by outside forces and, in the days of steam, snail-like as the iron wheels struggled for traction in rising and falling crescendos.

> *Forty years ago. On the platform of Amiens Street Station smelling of midnight dust, fish, steam, petrol. The two of them joking upwards to the two girls in the lighted carriage, holding their hands until the very last moment when the engine shook itself and chugged slowly out. Then two white hands waving back through the steam until train and lights and hands vanished around the curve like falling cards.*
> Sean O'Faolain – *Hymeneal* [3]

All of this is gone.

In his book, *Forgotten Railways of Scotland*, J Thomas aptly refers to the line closures of the 1950s and 1960s as *'clearances'*. The methods employed during the land clearances may have been more shocking, but there are parallels with the long-term impact for isolated communities. Alas, be they bankers or government ministers, those responsible line their pockets and walk away scot-free; may they never rest. There is surely a place in the modern world for the return of the evil eye and ill-wishers once prevalent in the Highlands.

Significantly, Killin Station was not the end of the line, because it continued north across a bridge over the Lochay, veered eastwards near Finlarig Castle and the golf course, running parallel to Pier Road and terminating at Loch Tay where there once stood a small station and a single, cramped engine shed. The line continued from the station onto the pier enabling a direct connection with the Loch Tay Steamers which headed east to Kenmore via Ardeonaig, Lawers, Ardtalnaig and Fearnan.

The Loch Tay Steam Company was established by the Earl of Breadalbane in 1882 and survived in various hands until 1949, ten years longer than Loch Tay Station, which closed for passengers on the eve of the Second World War. The first steamer to ply Loch Tay was the 92 foot *Lady of the Lake* capable of carrying 100 passengers. This was followed by the *Queen of the Lake* and then by two cargo vessels, the *Carlotta* and the *Sybilla* – the former named after the Earl's wife and the latter after Queen Sybilla, who died in 1122 on the tiny island of Eilean nam Ban (isle of the female saints) at the eastern end of Loch Tay. In its early years the golf course was thus served by rail from the west and water from the east. The Earl of Breadalbane not only owned the steamship company but was instrumental in bringing the railway to Killin in 1886 and subsequently in 1918, ensuring the golf course continued to exist on land convenient to both. The Earl, or to give him his full title, Sir Gavin Campbell, 7th Earl of Breadalbane, 1st Marquess of Breadalbane KG, PC, JP, DL, is the primary reason Killin has a golf course.

It is approached down a short lane leading to the car park and the clubhouse, which, despite the honesty box, has always been manned by welcoming bar staff on each of my three visits; may there be many more. The first tee is found on the left of the approach road about 100 yards from the clubhouse. This picturesque par 4 hugs the banks of the Lochay and there must be golf balls aplenty resting on its banks as a pushed drive sliding to the right is too easily lost to its waters. The new tenth tee is further up the approach road and is a more daunting proposition, playing over the swirling waters of an inlet formed by a sharp bend in the river.

From either location it is a tantalising opener, particularly as 175 yards down, a ditch traverses the fairway. To drive the ditch or lay up, *to die, to sleep; To sleep: perchance to dream: ay there's the rub* [4] – a major decision and the round has only just begun. As you walk the fairway to determine your drive's final resting place, you can take solace from the view to your right where river and glen converge on the single-track bridge with its high stone arch dating from the late eighteenth century. Killin has many a compensation, regardless of the quality of your golf.

After the first green the course turns sharp left towards a pair of relatively straightforward par 3s up and down a gentle slope. To the right of the second fairway there is an avenue of trees which once formed an entrance into Finlarig Farm. The road into the golf course, running parallel to the first and crossing the second in front of the tee box, was once the primary route to the farm. It is therefore unsurprising that the early history of the club gave rise to various disputes with the tenants, Mr and Mrs Steen, although they were initially enthusiastic. The Royal and Ancient records for the club indicate that it was formed in 1911. Thus the official centenary was celebrated in 2011. However, the first mention of a golf course at Killin appears in newspapers from 1902, indicating that it officially opened on 13th June of that year –

the course is even marked on the Ordnance Survey map of the period. Precisely what happened in the intervening years is unclear, but it seems that by 1910 it had been abandoned[5] and it was not until 4th June 1914 that the course was finally reinstated by the said Mrs Steen and the first ball struck. Three weeks later, on 28th June, Archduke Franz Ferdinand of Austria was assassinated and Europe thrown into turmoil. By 1917 it had become impossible to maintain the course and it was at this stage Mr Steen proposed that it revert to agricultural use. His enthusiasm for golf had evidently waned, presumably because experience had taught him that ploughing the land was more profitable than the income he derived from the course, this despite being entitled to 98 per cent of the annual takings. It was only by appealing to the Earl of Breadalbane that the course was saved and the responsibility for its upkeep transferred to the members. It would be another thirty years before the club was finally able to purchase the land from the Breadalbane Estate, around the same time the Breadalbane Hydro Scheme started. This caused more problems for the club when construction lorries started using the old road through the course in preference to Pier Road where Black Bridge was deemed unsafe for heavy traffic – looking at what remains of the road through the course now it is hard to imagine how golf and heavy vehicles could possibly co-exist in such close proximity.

The wall through the third green marks the boundary with the old road into the estate and from here it is a sharp right to the fourth tee, *The Gully*, where things start to get serious. This stroke index 1 hole is 370 yards and the longest par 4 on the course. It comprises three sections: a hill, a plateau and another hill. The first shot is blind up to the plateau and the second shot to the green is also blind. On the left is harsh rough on a steep embankment and to the right trees with yet more punishing rough; it is a difficult hole. Across the top of the course the short par 3 fifth, *The Dyke*, is protected by a drystone wall to the front and bunkers back and to the sides; there really is no alternative but to go for the heart of the green. On the back nine a new raised tee to the left takes the drystone wall out of play but nothing else – named *Centenary*, appropriately it is 100 yards off all the tees.

The sixth, from its elevated tee almost outside the course, takes you part way back down the hill and the seventh brings you back again. The par 3 eighth shares the same elevated tee as the sixth, providing a close encounter with out-of-bounds for its entire length to the east. This crow's nest tee box will appeal to anyone who has been on a cruise ship with a 'driving range' and left feeling short changed, convinced that cruise companies are missing a trick. Any golfer would pay handsomely to drive from the top deck out to sea – balls made from fish food would serve a dual purpose.

Killin saves its best for the last. The par 5 ninth, *Home*, is over 500 yards downhill all the way back to the clubhouse. The temptation is to let rip from the tee box as the view towards Glen Lochay and Sròn a Chlachain looks so inviting, but be warned that anything leaking right will find trouble. The club understandably claims that this is *the most beautiful 9-hole course in Scotland*. I would find it difficult to assign this description to any course as there is such a rich variation of landscape even in the small number of courses visited in this book; beauty is in the eye of the beholder. However, for me the ninth/eighteenth at Killin can legitimately claim to be by far and away the best par 5; a spectacular finish to any course, nine or eighteen. This is a wonderful golf course which is always well presented despite the strains that must be placed on the greens' machinery by the steeply sloping terrain. In common with all of the courses in this book, I wonder how the fairways and greens were originally carved from the landscape and, more importantly, how they were subsequently maintained. I suspect our golfing ancestors were more tolerant of heavy rough and less than pristine fairways. Perhaps they were just better golfers and knew how to keep out of trouble, which, judging by the golf clubs of the time, they were obliged to achieve with very primitive equipment. The solution for many clubs was to allow sheep to graze the land while fencing off the greens, but there is no mention of this in the club's history. One particular event at Killin, as detailed in Gillean Ford's history of the club, provides an interesting insight into the perils of life on the original Committee. A note appears in the old minutes to the effect that *'the horse having contracted parasitic mange the Green Committee has had it destroyed'*. The Club was then summoned to appear within the Sheriff Court House, Dunblane, for failure *'to report with practicable speed that the horse had parasitic mange'*. They were fined ten shillings. The Committee was later given permission to *'purchase a Horse at a sum not exceeding £20'*.[6] My recent experience of sitting on a similar committee is much less exciting, although the scope of work under discussion is perhaps more comprehensive – elsewhere in Gillean Ford's history there is mention of *'hiring a tractor to cut the fairways at least four times per season'*, although this was 1945 when best intentions were probably constrained by lack of available resources, for example, fuel.

I am sure there are equivalent stories throughout the history of the Allendale course when the provision of a playing surface was a good deal more agriculturally biased than now. Before the move to High Studdon, Allendale Golf Club was sited at Thornley Gate where the contract with the farmer who owned the land allowed for the grazing of sheep and cattle and restricted the width of all fairways to just twenty-two yards; no other cutting was allowed. Thus, the fairways were lined with deep, ball-swallowing rough that varied in height dependent on the grazing habits of the resident animals. There was no intermediate semi-rough, it was all or nothing. Everything, including the rough, thrived on the constant supply of manure which also littered the fairways but not the greens; these were protected by an electrified fence erected at just the wrong height for the male members. I can find no evidence of visitors suing the club for personal damages.

The Killin clubhouse is a friendly, warm place which is manned seven days a week from April to the end of October. An active bar is a great asset to any club but the location and footfall for many similar-sized organisations are such that income rarely exceeds overheads except for special prearranged occasions. Killin could probably teach other clubs a thing or two.

Although enlarged and extended, the core of the clubhouse dates back to 1922 and above the bar there are pictures that bear testament to a long tradition of golf on the banks of the Lochay. There is the hand-forged *Captains' Special Putting Cleek* made by Robert Simpson of Carnoustie and strung with small medals of the winners since 1984. There is a picture from an exhibition match held in 1963 to mark the club's fiftieth anniversary and there are photographs of local dignitaries on the veranda at the opening of the clubhouse on 8th July 1922, a most unlikely-looking set of golfers.[7]

The picture of John Graham Wilson driving off in heavy tweeds and plus fours is a reminder of how much golf fashions have transformed into the practical since the early twentieth century.

Bearing in mind his contribution to the founding of the club, it is a pity that the Earl of Breadalbane was not present at the opening ceremony as within four months he died, aged seventy-one, at the Central Station Hotel, Glasgow while attending a meeting of railway directors. He was buried five days later on 24th October 1922 at Finlarig Castle, a short 300-yard walk from the second green along the old drive into the estate. Near to his railway, his steamship pier and his golf course, it is nevertheless a bleak place to rest. Sir Gavin Campbell at least has his wife, Lady Alma Imogen Leonora Carlotta Graham, for company, the last of the Breadalbanes; you would not want to spend the long dark nights of the soul alone in this place.

Adjacent to the graves are the ruined mausoleum, the shadow of the crumbling castle and the beheading pit used by his ancestor 'Black Duncan', the man with the incurable slice. Imprisoned noblemen were beheaded while commoners suffered the noose from a nearby oak tree. The belief that the castle is haunted seems entirely credible.

Notes

1. This quote from Garrison Keillor's *95 Theses 95* – from the *Lake Wobegone Days* collection.

2. The picture of Killin Station is from the G H Robin collection and is reproduced by courtesy of the Mitchell Library, Glasgow City Council.

3. This quote from Sean O'Faolain's 'Hymeneal' – a short story from his *The Talking Trees and Other Stories* collection – reprinted in the Penguin Modern Classic *Sean O'Faolain – Foreign Affairs and Other Stories*.

4.   William Shakespeare's *Hamlet* – Act 3 Scene 1.

5.   The *Glasgow Evening Times* of 31st March 1910 states: '*A course was in exist-ence a few years ago but owing to certain reasons it had to be abandoned*' – from the *History of Killin Golf Club 1902 – 2011* by Gillean Ford.

6.   From the *History of Killin Golf Club 1902 – 2011* by Gillean Ford.

7.   These pictures are reproduced by kind permission of Killin Golf Club.

To the West

It's never too late or, in my case, too early to be whatever you want to be. Benjamin Button's letter to his daughter.[1]

If my parents are responsible for my lack of putting prowess then it is my grandfather I must blame for my obsession with motor sport, at least in the sense that nobody else in the family tree had ever shown the slightest interest. Fred, by contrast, had competed on two wheels and four.

At a crucial point in my education I was entirely distracted by racing dreams and worked every available holiday to raise the funds for my first car. I was still sixteen when it was acquired so that on my seventeenth birthday Dad could take me for my first lesson when I behaved impeccably and continued to do so until I passed my test and then, never again since. My Austin Mini 850 was sky blue to match the colour of my aspirations. Lacking the funds to race on a track, I 'competed' on the Queen's highway. The car sported a large number of spotlights in the rallying fashion of the day, some operational, some not. It was shod in Michelin ZX radials which I could squeal on any corner of any radius. The steering wheel was raked down and the seats shifted back so far I was driving from a semi-recumbent position near the boot; and it was 'stripped down', anything superfluous was discarded. The first accident was not long coming – on the way to an icy Mallory Park Boxing Day race meeting I squared the front wheels and shifted the sub-frame back several inches in a collision with a roundabout on the Derby ring road. I confess I was out of control and I never really slowed down until a head-on crash in my early forties. I wrote off two cars at once, mine and the one coming the other way but both were company cars and therefore purpose built for such incidents. I climbed from that wreckage with no more than bruised ribs, hired a car and was only a few hours late for work, thereby ensuring my employer lost no revenue. Some years later the directors sold the company from under us and disappeared without so much as a fare-well or thanks – you live and learn, there would be a distinct advantage to lives lived in reverse.

I should always have been on a track where the danger to myself and others could have been limited but Dad was an industrial chemist not a garage owner, nor a farmer with a field to practise on. It was in the blood but too far back and on the wrong side of the family. Dad should have been a garage owner from Dumbuck or a farmer from Duns. Nevertheless, late in life I have made a wonderful discovery; *riding a motorcycle has a lot in common with driving a racing car. It requires 100% concentration at all times, you must be constantly reading the road, you are wearing a helmet and when you get it wrong, the conse-quences can be painful.*[2] Just like Toad, I am now to be seen hurtling around the back roads of Northumberland; once again I can blame Fred. And this is the strangest thing, it is something like playing golf, which also demands 100 per cent concentration – any average golfer can sneak the odd gross par or birdie, but to do that consistently across eighteen holes demands total dedication to the task. Riding a bike is the same, let your mind wander and the consequences can be signifi-cantly worse than a triple bogey. The idea of combining *Golf in the Wild* with a motorcycle tour is appealing, but one that must wait for a solution to the difficulty of transporting golf clubs. As I head north through Killin, for the time being at least, I remain on four wheels.

*

The road through the village climbs gently towards the Falls of Dochart and the twisted bridge which crosses the river and the small downstream island, Innis Bhuidhe, home to the Clan MacNab Burial Ground. The road then climbs 2 miles towards Glen Ogle, Lix Toll and the junction with the A85 to Crianlarich and Oban. The road to Lix Toll runs parallel with the former Killin branch line where it joined the *Callandar and Oban Line* at Killin Junction, just over a mile west of the road junction.

The branch line closed on 27th September 1965, five months ahead of Beeching's schedule, following a landslide the previous day at Gleno- gle that stopped all mainline traffic. Since then, the only option has been to drive the 11 miles along the A85 from Lix Toll to Crianlarich where you can play the old steam train enthusiast's game of *'spot the dismantled railway'*, the old mainline following the road throughout its journey along Glen Dochart. On the northern side of the road is the River Dochart, followed by Loch Iubhair and then Loch Dochart where on a wooded island perches another of Black Duncan's resi- dences, Loch Dochart Castle.

From Crianlarich the direct and obvious route is to head due west, but there is an alternative and more exciting road that follows the West Highland Line 16 miles south through Ardlui to Tarbet and the junc- tion with the A83, which follows the path of the old military road to Inveraray and Loch Fyne. Circling Arrochar, the top of Loch Long and passing the old torpedo testing site, the road heads northwest up Glen Croe. For centuries this route has been known as the *Rest And Be Thankful*. The road has its origins in the Jacobite uprisings when Gen- eral George Wade recommended establishment of military bases inter- connected by Highland roads such that troops could be moved quickly and conveniently between locations to quell any local uprisings. The General's Inspector of Roads, Major Caulfield, first surveyed the route in 1743, and by 1748 the road over the Glen Croe summit was com- pleted by troops from the 24th Regiment, who erected a stone seat with the legend *'Rest And Be Thankful'*. The remainder of the road down to Loch Fyne was completed in 1749. The modern day A83 eventually replaced the original single-track highway at the end of the 1930s, and as you drive along the southwestern flank of Ben Arthur, stretches of the original route can be seen below on the floor of the

Glen. While the modern version ascends gradually by cutting a route along the mountainside, the original delays the steep ascent to the last. This had glorious consequences.

In 1949 the Royal Scottish Automobile Club (RSAC) used the final 1-mile ascent of the Wade-Caulfield route to establish the magnificent *Rest And Be Thankful* hillclimb, an event which continued almost uninterrupted for another twenty years. Jackie Stewart describes this place as *'the cradle of my life in motor racing'* (*Winning is Not Enough*, his autobiography from 2007), first as a spectator, watching his elder brother Jim compete in his Healey Silverstone and later, in July 1961, as a competitor in a Ford-powered Marcos. Stewart has fond memories of these times, *'the public address announcer shouting out the names of the drivers and their cars and all their split times and his voice would echo down the Glen and I used to sit there wide-eyed enjoying a spectacle as thrilling and exhilarating as any young boy could imagine, hardly daring to blink'*; and so in the shadow of Ben Arthur began the drive to fame, fortune and the career-long dance with death and tragedy.

From the A83, the old road looks innocuous, but in that last mile it rises over 400 feet creating a hill climb as challenging as any in Europe. Archive newsreel from the 1950 event projects a diverse array of machinery, mostly pre-war and pre-conformity, the only design constraints being the imagination. Dennis Poore in the monstrous flying Pegasus bi-wheeled 4.5 litre Alfa 8C-35, Raymond Mays and Ken Wharton in ERAs and Basil Davenport in the skinny GN Spider, all forward and trust in the Lord, a seriously strange but effective device dating from the early 1920s in which the driver appears to sit astride the car in homage to its cyclecar origins. All arms and elbows, they attack Stonebridge, Cobblers and the Hairpin with true grit, determination – and no protection.

In July 1958 Jim Clark competed here in both a Porsche 1600S and a Triumph TR3, finishing first and second respectively. On his way home he called on his friend Jim Stewart at Dumbuck Garage where his younger brother Jackie raced out of the house eager to see this rising star. It would be 1962 before they were formally introduced at Charterhall and from that moment their lives were intertwined, until that fateful day at Hockenheim on 7th April 1968.

By the time I travelled to Silverstone for the 1969 British Grand Prix on 19th July it seemed the world had moved on more than 365 days from the 1968 event. The era-defining combination of Clark and Chapman had been replaced by Stewart and Tyrrell, the grids were fuller, elevated wings banned and the racing tighter; the magnificent duel in the sun between Stewart and Rindt only being interrupted by the fragility of the Lotus 49B. Overhead shots of the pair drifting through Woodcote show machinery flexing sideways, teetering on the edge, at the very pinnacle of man in harmony with machine. The next day, *the very next day*, man and machine went further than ever before, the Eagle landed in the Sea of Tranquillity, man had arrived on the moon. The space programme that gave birth to the microprocessor marked the real beginnings of the computer age. As I drifted towards my own sea of tranquillity, for good or for worse, our futures were being mapped out.

Much remains of the original hill climb section, although various gates prevent any unauthorised adventures which, given the challenging nature of the last quarter mile, is probably no bad thing. Where once the tarmac was rutted, covered in loose grit and narrowed by encroaching vegetation, it is now mysteriously pristine and once more awaiting the feel of hot rubber – perhaps competitive motor sport will once again return to this hallowed place.

In 2003 Motor Sport's Gordon Cruickshank wrote an entertaining Track Test of the climb and discovered that the burger van at the summit car park was run by Dario Franchitti's[3] uncle. The current incumbent thought me a little mad when I tried to make the same connection. Sadly, even that link with the world of racing has now gone. From the summit of the Rest, the long descent to Loch Fyne is less severe but no less spectacular. The A83 follows the route of the original military road but without the incentive for preservation provided by the RSAC, it is much less evident. The road loops around the north end of the Loch and then keeps close company with its shores through to Inveraray where it narrows at Aray Bridge, sharply ascends and descends the humped rise into the new town. 'New' can be a relative term and certainly Inveraray has nothing in common with Milton Keynes.

Inveraray Castle, which looks more like a Loire Valley chateau, sits just inland from where the River Aray flows into the Loch. In 1744 Archibald Campbell 3rd Duke of Argyll decided to demolish the original castle and replace it with an imposing new mansion. Any such building demands landscaped gardens and arresting views, the only problem being that the old town standing adjacent to the castle presented a formidable blot on the landscape. No matter, the town was demolished to satisfy the Duke's desires and a new town established where his sensibilities would not be offended. The two fortunate by-products of his wishes were that the rebuilt town is one of the most delightful and unusual small towns in Scotland and, in 1893, the castle grounds became home to the town golf course.

Notes

1. A quote from: *The Curious Case of Benjamin Button*, a 2008 American fantasy film directed by David Fincher. The film is loosely based on the 1922 short story of the same name by F. Scott Fitzgerald. The quote continues: *'There's no time limit, stop whenever you want. You can change or stay the same, there are no rules to this thing'*. Benjamin Button lives his life backwards.

2. Based on observations by Martin Brundle in *Motor Sport*, Vol. 88 No. 12 – December 2012 Edition

3. Dario Franchitti is a Scottish racing driver based in America – a multiple race winner, his outstanding achievement is being three times victorious at the Indianapolis 500.

Inveraray

Scotland, I rush towards you, into my future that, every minute, grows smaller and smaller. Norman MacCaig – *London to Edinburgh*

The original Inveraray course in the grounds of the castle was opened in 1893, but, as with many golf courses, war brought temporary or permanent closure. The original course was closed at the start of the Second World War and the establishment of Combined Training Centre (CTC) Castle Camp ensured little remained by its end. Much in the way that the town was relocated by the 3rd Duke of Argyll on aesthetic considerations, the 10th and 11th descendants took a similarly dismal view of the great unwashed playing golf in the castle grounds. The course remained closed until 19th June 1993 when it was reopened by the 12th Duke at an appropriate distance from the castle, on the southern side of town. The date coincides with the club's centenary, although for fifty-four of those years there was no course, a period roughly equivalent to the time it took to relocate and rebuild the new town. Disrupting lives for the sake of the gentry would not be tolerated in the twenty-first century, but, by contrast, disrupting lives for golf seems to be acceptable, as Donald Trump has demonstrated on the east coast of Scotland. From the vantage point of an elevated ego, Trump looked down on the 'disgusting conditions' lived in by the locals. Peg looked down on everyone.

Nobody could escape my mother's critical eye, '*the good, the bad, the rich, the poor, the loveliest and the best*';[1] the family member, the close friend, the casual acquaintance, the distant cousin, Royalty, almost no one was exempt. The notable exceptions were the Queen Mother and, strangely, Prince Phillip with whom, in her dotage, she claimed a romantic entanglement. She also had visions of dead people standing in black at the foot of her bed – please protect me from this sad end.

The major exception was her father, Frederick Ernest Twinn. He was revered and consequently admired by us all; love rubs off. Born in Salisbury in 1891, his family moved to Andover in 1893 where the roots of his life took hold, a life enmeshed in motorbikes, cars, speed and, ultimately, flight. Apprenticed as a motor engineer after leaving school, he spent the rest of his life grubby and scar-handed, delving into engines and machinery. He acquired his first driving licence in December 1909 steering local buses along dusty Hampshire roads and, later, drove a wide range of army vehicles including the General's limousine. These are his words on the reverse of the postcard:

Dear Dad and Ma
I expect you can see who this is. I have had a couple of days
on this job again. Charles Miles told me I am in for 2 stripes.

I hope it comes off all right. I think we are moving away from here[2] about Wed – it was Monday at first. Hope all are well.

Love to all from
Fred
Drove the General in this on Saturday

Enlisted in the Terriers (Territorial Army), he was sent to Gallipoli in 1914 and then transferred to the Royal Flying Corps training school at Aboukir, Egypt, where he rose to the rank of Chief Mechanic. A collection of photographs from the time show Fred with a variety of wrecked aircraft, taking part in local 'Inter-Nation' football matches and posing in front of the Sphinx, whose inscrutable smile is much more evident than in the twenty-first century. I guess there was hardship but the overwhelming impression is of young men in their prime having the time of their lives, securely distant from the horror of the trenches. Fred stands proud and hatless in the centre with a folding roll film camera in his left hand, his pith helmet in his right and a

93

centre parting kept in place with a touch of pomade. Their guide takes centre stage while a white horse enters stage left and a caged chicken exits stage right. In the wings a herd of camel riders is gathering by a distant pyramid while the airmen stand patiently posing in the dry desert heat.

The science fiction world obsesses about time travel, but windows into earlier lives can be found in most attics, filed in boxes waiting for the light. This and our sense of smell can resurrect people and places we thought had gone forever. When I knew my grandfather he was a tapestry of reassuring odours, predominantly Brylcreem, Three Nuns tobacco and probably alcohol.

Fred was dispersed from Fovant Camp near Salisbury on 18th February 1919, his brother already gone.

Between the wars he continued to work in motor engineering and in his spare time took part in motorcycle trials, built a Lea Francis from two wrecked halves and raced at Brooklands. By combining his passion for cars with a keen interest in local football, Fred organised what was claimed to be the first floodlit football match in the country. He surrounded the pitch with automobiles and turned on their headlights, engines running to keep the batteries from going flat. It is a wonder the players did not collapse from carbon monoxide poisoning.

A full-time officer in the local fire brigade, he raised money for Andover's first ambulance and, during the Second World War, fought the blitz fires at Southampton and Portsmouth. After the war he worked as a fitter at a local engineering company and worked there until the day he died, aged seventy-six. Mum blamed her mother for having him work too hard in the garden and then continued to blame her for much else; 'nobody liked May' who I was taught to mistrust and dutifully called her Mrs Kipper. I did not like to be left alone in her company; disdain rubs off, too.

It seems likely that it was not a happy marriage and that digging in the garden, tending the greenhouse, feeding the chickens and nightly trips to the pub were just a means of escape. Add to this his organisation of the annual Andover Carnival, a significant event attracting celebrities of the day, and it would seem May spent many hours alone and embittered. I do not remember the origins of 'Mrs Kipper', but, whereas my grandfather emanated warmth and reassurance, Florence May gave off an earthier, less attractive odour. I would have taken my mother's propaganda as gospel; they were permanently at war.

Born in 1896, Florence was five years younger than Fred, who she married in 1921. Anyone who loved her called her Florence so I never heard her called anything other than May. I remember her as a small, plump old lady with a deeply lined face, a blue hat permanently anchored to her head and slightly bandy legs which gave her an unstable sideways waddle rather than a walk; she trod a very uncertain path. At the time of my earliest memories she would have been under sixty.

Florence never received a good press in the family. Always labelled as mean and ill-tempered, now I wonder if somehow cause and effect became inverted. She died in 1968 and my sister remembers that, in her last days, she lay on her deathbed refusing to open her eyes to the family, determined to continue her uncertain path, alone to the end.

I remember that she was partial to a bottle of Mackeson stout which Fred would bring home fresh from the pub every evening; I remember she spoke with a broad Hampshire accent and she could never place people's names – everyone was referred to as 'old wotsizname', so that if more than one such person occurred in a sentence, all meaning was lost. And this is the saddest part; Florence May was once a very pretty young girl with a kind face and a bright future. Whatever followed, it seems certain that those closest to her could have been kinder. The bright young thing that won the heart of the dashing Fred had long since gone when I was a boy.

Fred's life reads like a Michael Palin Ripping Yarn, a life not possible in this globalised risk-averse century where most adventures are either no longer original or beyond the means of all but the filthy rich, the unhinged and the obsessed. There was so much more scope for ordinary people to do extraordinary things. I belong to a generation almost entirely insulated from the impact of war. Except those obliged by circumstance or ambition to take up arms, the machinations of war-obsessed governments go largely unpunished. By stark contrast, long stretches of my parents' and grandparents' lives were acutely influenced by conflict.

Nobody was immune, even the most far-flung communities had their part to play, not to mention the sacrifices etched on countless village war memorials. On the road to Inveraray on the western shore of Loch Long, opposite the village of Arrochar, stands the half-demolished remains of the Royal Navy Torpedo Testing Station which was operational from April 1912 to December 1986. These unguided devices required 3,000 yards of clear water and the relatively shallow upper reaches of Loch Long were ideally suited to testing speed, depth, consistency and straight line accuracy. Unarmed torpedoes were fired at floating targets down the Loch from tubes beneath the test facility pier or from a Clyde Puffer specially modified for the task. After the torpedo was recovered by one of seven boats, it would be adjusted and retested as many as five times until deemed fit for issue to the Royal Navy. From 1936 the torpedoes were manufactured locally at the Alexandria Royal Naval Torpedo factory just south of Loch Lomond, in the palatial factory built for the ill-fated Argyll Motors Ltd; its grandiose frontage remains to this day. At its peak in 1944, in excess of 12,000 torpedoes were fired down the Loch at an average of 48 per day. Lethal instruments of destruction born of such peaceful waters.

To the west, at Loch Fyne and Inveraray, there was even more intense activity. It is remarkable to consider that in 1940, following the fall of France and retreat from Dunkirk, politicians and military planners were not just focussed on defence and the potential German invasion but also the special training required for invasion by sea and the eventual retaking of France. Inveraray was immediately established as Number 1 Combined Training Centre (No. 001 CTC). Six camps were built in and around Inveraray as well as the Naval Camp known as HMS *Quebec*. In the Loch there were an array of permanently moored warships, including two Mississippi river boats, and regular visits from naval ships and units from the Allied fleets. In the period from 1940 to 1944, around a quarter of a million allied servicemen from all three forces were trained there; the D-Day landings effectively began in and around Inveraray. The small town consequently attracted some very high-ranking visitors including King George VI, General de Gaulle and Winston Churchill, much elevated from his 1918 position of Secretary of State for the Royal Air Force. A roll of honour and a collection of pictures once displayed in the Loch Fyne

Hotel have been removed by a previous owner for private consumption. All that remains is a picture of King George VI standing outside the hotel entrance in the autumn of 1941.

INVERARAY AND LOCH FYNE.

The new course resides on Argyll Estate land once occupied by CTC Avenue and Town camps, which explains the reinforced concrete driveway and car park, originally constructed to bear heavy armoury. The aerial postcard view dates from around 1910 and appears to show a course either side of the river in a quite majestic setting. The new course is about a mile due south of the castle. This is not a pristine course, but it has character, retaining some evidence of its recent history; it is at some remove from the artificially manicured corporate enclaves which seek no relationship to their surroundings. The first is a good example: a short 121-yard friendly opener to a slightly elevated green where, to the right, is located the brick remains of CTC Avenue Camp Cook House after which the hole is named. The second, a blind 280-yard par 4 between trees, heads north towards the town and introduces a problem that occurs on some of the other fairways. My first visit followed a particularly wet winter and the ground had become overly receptive. So much so that my first drive was never seen again, the ball plugged deep in Mother Earth. The subsoil is primarily peat and clay which generates a too-absorbent surface and a lower layer which does not drain adequately. Bearing in mind that this land was home to a military camp during the Second World War it is likely that the subsoil is compacted, making drainage worse than it might be under normal circumstances. This is *Golf in the Wild*, not a tour around Augusta National; I am not seeking perfection.

The third, *The Hedges*, is the obligatory 491-yard par 5 which is played towards the iconic 126-foot Inveraray Bell Tower, built to commemorate the Clan Campbell dead from the First World War. The bells were delivered in 1921 via the original *Rest and Be Thankful* road and took two attempts to reach the summit, no doubt having enormous difficulty negotiating the hairpin – it is a wonder they were delivered at all.

The green sits at the furthest point north on the course, the fairway running parallel to an *Area of Archaeological Significance* which contains round cairns dating from the Bronze Age, the humble origins of my Ping Anser manganese bronze putter. This was a bargain second hand club dating from the 1960s and is the only device which can deliver some hint of reliability to my putting stroke. The putter *tarnishes with age to create a distinctive look that symbolizes confidence and trust* – really! Perhaps I should stop cleaning it. After the 2012 Masters, Lee Westwood sacked his putting coach following some dismal statistics on the National's greens. I blame my parents, he blames his coach, in the modern world the buck never stops being passed.

I understand the secret to golfing success is practice: *'the harder I practice the luckier I get'*, to quote that well-worn phrase attributed to Gary Player. The problem with practice is that it is tedious and it takes a particularly obsessive one-dimensional personality to persist; by way of example, Lee Westwood is apparently proud to claim that he has never read a book, presumably too busy refining his putting stroke.

Before I ventured onto a golf course I spent many long hours at the driving range perfecting my skills at hitting a golf ball off a nicely resistant, solid green mat. When I finally ventured out onto the real thing, it all came as something of a shock and disappointment. Real tees and real fairways, particularly the damp ones of Northumberland, don't offer the same rebound qualities as plastic on concrete and so my irons dug firmly in the turf and the ball flew off in a wide variety of directions, never the one intended. I occasionally visit the driving range for the sheer joy of thrashing a ball without consequence, but rarely do I derive any benefit.

I don't know if the poets Paul Farley and Mike Symmons Roberts are golfers, but their analysis of the out-of-town floodlit driving range is pitch-perfect:

> *This isn't about golf at all. The range ritual has more in common with yoga or dance than it has with golf. You come away having helped to make great shapes in the floodlit sky. Your role in this was to turn up, receive your basket of shiny white objects, then propel them out into the ether. Once you have sent them all on their way, you step aside, and someone else will take your bay. The volunteers change throughout the night, but this ritual pattern-making, continues. If this had been dreamt up by Mark Wallinger or Gillian Wearing it would be in the running for the Turner Prize –* from their jointly authored book, *Edgelands*.

Real aficionados should head down to the Golf Club at Chelsea Piers, Manhattan's multi-tiered driving range:

No buckets of golf balls here! The Golf Club's driving range uses a Computee RC20000 series automatic ball tee-up system designed by Sunaga Kihatsu of Japan. Purchase a ball card, insert it into your hitting stall's card reader, and golf balls begin to tee-up. Instructors work with golfers of all levels to improve techniques and strategies and to build confident mental attitudes.[3]

You then have the privileged illusion of thrashing the shiny white objects into the Hudson River. Putting all ideas of *'thrashing shiny objects'* out of my head, I approach the next tee, with a *'confident mental attitude'* remembering to 'let the club do the work' – if only it were that easy. The fourth, *Riochan,* is a testing 355-yard par 4 with houses to the left and a parallel long ditch to the right. This leads to a short blind par 4 over a ridge to a green tucked in a corner and protected by a pond. On a drier day this would be a very pleasing hole, but, like the second, a too receptive fairway swallowed my ball whole and the blind tee shot offered no hint of where it may be hiding. A short par 3 leads up hill to a sloping green protected on three sides by mature trees, a copse which is clearly visible from RAF aerial photographs of the CTC Avenue Camp taken in December 1942.

The seventh, *Fyne View,* certainly is and I judge it my favourite on the course. The drive out of the copse is tight but rewarding as you progress down the 380-yard fairway to the green adjacent to the road, the lowest point on the course. The second shot crosses an unadopted section of *The Avenue*, an historic feature which stretches from the centre of town to the golf club's entrance. The Avenue's beech trees, planted in 1650, separated the Duke of Argyll's estate from the land where the new town of Inveraray was eventually built. The neat positioning of the green, the downhill fairway and the Loch Fyne panorama conspire to make this a very satisfying golf hole.

The eighth climbs back up the hill along a 390-yard fairway to a green neatly protected by a dry stone wall at just about the point where my second shot would start its descent; I laid up and hit the green with my third – a shame about the subsequent three putt. The ninth, *Twin Oaks,* takes you downhill and home to a sloping green protected by the aforementioned trees; the second shot has to be straight and true. Inveraray is a neat course with all of the right components – an interesting history, an honesty box, a generous par 5, some friendly par 3 holes, fine views and no pretentions. There is no 'old guard' watching your every move for a careless misdemeanour. Ties and jackets are not compulsory in the clubhouse; there isn't one.

Notes

1. This should be attributed to Bob Dylan who included the *'loveliest and the best'* in the title track of his 2012 album, *Tempest*. I then discovered that he, in turn, had borrowed the phrase from Edward FitzGerald's translation of *The Rubaiyat of Omar Khayyam*. *The Tempest* is, in turn, a reworking of the Carter Family's song, *Titanic*.

2. *'here'* I am guessing is the Fovant Dispersal Camp near Salisbury, the place he would return to in February 1919 at the end of the First World War

3. From *The Golf Club at Chelsea Piers* website – www.chelseapiers.com

To Mull

The sixties began in the summer of 1956, ended in October of 1973 and peaked just before dawn on 1st July 1967. Joe Boyd[1]

I was born too late. My sixties began on 25th April 1969, ended on 6th October 1973 and peaked as I made my way to London, Whittington-like, in April 1971.

There are places that belong to us; the happy hours spent at Oulton Park inhaling Castrol R throughout the mid-to late sixties were mostly observed from the stand at Lodge Corner. The top right terrace was ours and provided perfect line of sight for cars emerging from Druids, braking hard into Lodge, drifting through the exit before plunging into Deer's Leap. Nobody did it better than Chris Amon in an F1 Ferrari 312, inch perfect every time. It was a wonderful test – the apex sat in a dip and was invisible until you were on it; the exit began on the entry into Deer's Leap before the corner had ended so those on the limit were sitting in a car which looked high on its suspension and too light on its feet. It was easy to see who was trying and who wasn't. The grandstand no longer exists, having been demolished to make way for a gravel trap. More progress in the name of safety.

If you spend any time in one place with people of a common inter-est friendships soon develop. There was a group of about a dozen people who regularly gathered at Lodge Corner, reserving 'our patch' with folding garden chairs much as a German will use a beach towel. Our own cars parked to the rear of the stand position us precisely in automotive history: an 'Austin Seven' Mini 850, a Cortina GT (in the colour scheme of the Lotus variant), an Austin 1100, a Vauxhall Viva, a 'new' Fiat 128 and a Sunbeam Rally Imp of very questionable reli-ability. It was in the Cortina GT that I was taken to Brands Hatch for the BOAC 500 long-distance Sports Car Championship race on 13th April 1969 to see Jo Siffert and Brian Redman run away from the opposition in a Porsche 908. Redman, from Colne in Lancashire, was an Oulton Park hero, along with Brian Classic who was one of the first to acquire Derek Bennett's Chevron B1, built in a mill in Bolton and a precursor to a dynasty of highly successful racing sports cars; we were defiantly northern in our tastes. Both Brians were involved in life-threatening incidents but both lived to tell the tale. Redman had three major accidents including one at St Jovite in Canada where the local press had pronounced him dead. He continued racing because, from his experience, the really big accidents didn't hurt, so why stop.

The trip to Brands was in the company of two Lodge Corner friends from Blackburn whose first love was rallying. Both were employees of Mullard and enthusiastic members of the Mullard Motor Cycle & Car Club, the MMCCC which, when translated from the equivalent Roman numerals, becomes the 2300 Club. It still exists but with a significantly reduced membership. Much of the conversation throughout 1969 was their planned trip to Scotland for the inaugural *Tour of Mull Rally*, an event which continues to this day, the 2300 Club only relinquishing its organisational responsibility to the Mull Car Club in 2010. Forty-three years later I follow in their enthusiastic footsteps and head for the island, except the motivation is golf and not speed, something my seventeen-year-old self would find hard to comprehend.

It is a short drive from Inveraray to Oban and the Caledonian Mac-Brayne ferry. Retracing the road back into the town, the route north is along the A819 which is left at The Argyll Hotel, under the arch. It is one of a series which interconnect the buildings along Front Street. The road climbs Glen Aray for 15 miles emerging on the southern shores of Loch Awe before connecting with the Crianlarich to Oban road west of Dalmally.

A few miles west is the village of Taynuilt. The heart of the community is off the main A85, a right turn heading north to a jetty that once provided the main ferry route north to Bonawe and beyond. The narrow empty slipway reaches out into Loch Etive without purpose, built at a time when cars were slim and balanced on tyres not much wider than you find on a Raleigh bicycle. I was tempted down this road by the sign at the A85 junction – Raon-Goilf – Golf Course. Somehow this backwater had passed me by during my research so I felt obliged to investigate, just to see what might be there you understand; just to park up and have a quick look. Then the sun came out, the course was empty, the broom was in flower and the fairways looked so neat that I could not resist – a 9-hole fix for a weary traveller. Taynuilt was a pleasant diversion; the entrance is unprepossessing, surrounded as it is by a small sports facility and football pitch, but once across the narrow bridge into the car park it is evident that this is a much cared-for course with an apparently new clubhouse, stone walls and tidy borders; the drive down the first is irresistible. The great attraction for the over-golfed weary traveller is that the course is almost entirely on the level. Squeezed into what must be the few acres of flatland for miles, it gives the impression of sitting at the foot of towering alpine mountains, enclosed on three sides; it is a wonderful setting.

Neither are there too many nasty surprises for the uninitiated, the least obvious threat coming from a series of ditches which traverse and surround some of the fairways. There is an explanatory map on the reverse of the golf card but I am a great believer in playing blind, a philosophy akin to ignoring manuals that accompany electrical goods. Fear is my ever-present companion on the golf course, so what I don't know about cannot concern me. Planning my way around the course, having the accuracy demanded to avoid trouble are attributes not to be found in my golf bag, better to hit and hope and claim ignorance – *'who on earth thought putting a bunker there was a good idea!'*

As it turned out, my 'blind' approach worked well – most trouble is fairly visible, only the third par 3, *Brolas*, demanding some close inspection with a ditch that comes into play the nearer you get to the green – I chickened out and went a few yards left looking for the up and down that didn't come. There is no par 5 but the 373-yard par 4 fourth, *Etive*, is a long hit down an incline and a good test of golf. Similarly, the shorter fifth, *Balindeor*, coming back up the hill, is a rewarding hole, but avoid the tree to the left which neatly blocks out the green. Holes one to seven play out in a friendly and welcoming manner, but the course has a sting in the tail which will catch the complacent. The 208-yard par 3 eighth has a narrow approach surrounded by trees – slice into the forestry and that neat card will begin to look very untidy as you hack your way towards the green. Similarly, the stroke index 1 dogleg left 9th, *Nant*, has the ability to wipe the smile from your face. There is out-of-bounds down the left and a line of trees to the right. The strong temptation is to go a fraction right as there is welcoming space beyond the tree line, but get behind them and the route to the impossibly small green may demand the use of a hard hat and body armour to avoid the ricochet. Despite the finish and despite the long walk in from the 9th, Taynuilt is an enjoyable diversion and a fine end as the long day closes towards Oban.

*

The road into Oban follows the single railway track line that opened from Dalmally in 1880, the final section of the Crianlarich and Oban Railway which terminates to the rear of the ferry terminal. The village of Connel sits on the banks of Loch Etive at the point where it narrows and connects with the Forth of Lorne a few miles east of Oban. The north and south shores are connected by Connel Bridge and the A85 passes beneath its stone arches.

Sometime during the summer days of 1955 a 'man of the road' stepped down from a lorry at Connel Bridge; it had been a welcome short lift. The lorry continued with its load of tar to Oban while the tramp headed north by foot across the bridge. I imagine him clean-shaven and well-presented, unlike his fellow travellers, unlike the man he would eventually become.[2]

In the 1950s the roads of southern England were awash with the shell-shocked and homeless of two world wars, ex-soldiers who had taken to the road from the desire or necessity to escape the rat-race or their nightmares. I remember them as a common sight on the chalk-lined dappled A roads of Berkshire and Hampshire as we journeyed south from Manchester to visit grandparents. I guess the majority chose the southern counties for the warmth and plentiful supply of villages and farms where most could expect a sympathetic reception; certainly on the rare occasion they appeared at home in Cheshire, my mother would always find something to give. This bereaved man of the road and ex-soldier was different though; the lorry had picked him up just beyond *Rest and Be Thankful* and he was heading in stages to the far north, as far as possible into the wild and away from his past. His name was James McRory Smith and, many days later, our paths would cross.

*

The bridge is not attractive; its angular steel in stark contrast to the stone arches at each end but it does have an odd history. It was built in 1903 as a railway bridge connecting the Oban line with the branch line between Connel and Ballachullish. Soon after its construction a railway wagon was used to ferry cars across the bridge and then in 1904 it became dual use, a road squeezed in next to the line to allow cars and trains to cross but not simultaneously. This dual use continued until 1966 when the Ballachullish line was closed and the bridge became dedicated to road transport; this, in turn, closed the ferry at Taynuilt. Three years later the 2300 Club members passed beneath its arches heading for the ferry and Mull. In 1969 this was a sizeable motor club drawn from Mullard Blackburn where 6,500 staff were employed in the construction of TV and radio valves, the largest manufacturing plant of its type in Europe. The mighty micro made this endeavour redundant; the 1969 moon landings marked endings as well as beginnings.

The Oban to Craignure ferry is the final step in the journey to Mull. This is a forty-five minute cruise across the waters of the Firth of Lorne and the southern reaches of the Sound of Mull. As the ferry leaves Oban, it passes between Alexander Carrick's War Memorial on the mainland to the east and the Isle of Kerrara to the west. The *Brothers in Arms* sculpture, erected in 1923, is considered to be Carrick's masterpiece and depicts a wounded soldier supported on each arm by his comrades; in turn their arms support his legs to form a cupped circle. Perhaps the composition symbolises the passing of time and how we are locked into an endless cycle of catastrophic repetition. It is reminiscent of Don McCullin's 1968 picture of an American marine supported by his brothers in arms, having been shot in both legs during the Têt offensive at Hué. Both sculpture and image have been compared to the crucifixion.

> *Years later I went back to Hué. It seemed so inconsequential, the whole thing. Those men who died, and those men who were maimed for life, went through all that, and it was totally futile, as all wars are known to be. Without profit, without horizons, without joy. I remember there was a street in Da Nang called Street without Joy. They could have called the whole country after that street* – Don McCullin – *Unreasonable Behaviour.*[3]

At the start of Second World War, across the waters in Ardentrive Bay on Kerrera, RAF Oban was home to a variety of Coastal Command flying boat squadrons, mostly piloting Short Sunderlands. In a repetition of 1914–18, it was expected that German u-boats would be used to attack Atlantic shipping convoys and Oban was ideally located for convoy escort and anti-submarine duties. The RAF personnel billeted in Oban's hotels would be familiar with Alexander Carrick's sculpture.

The Sunderlands were the largest aircraft of their time and must have made a stirring sight and sound rising from Oban Bay. With a wing-span of 113 feet, 85 feet in length and powered by 4 aero engines each developing in excess of 1,100bhp, they would leave the sea at around 85 to 90 knots. These were true flying boats, having no landing gear and only brought to shore for repair by slipways, like any other seaborne vessel. A squadron anchored in the bay floated like a flock of pterosaurs drying their wings; long since extinct, all that remains are the slipways at Ardentrive Bay and Ganavan Sands.

> *... on the wings of a flying boat a hundred gulls were holding a parliament, as they might have done in the wastes of the ocean, on Suliskeir or Rona.* Margaret Leigh, *Driftwood and Tangle*, writing about the Western Highlands in 1941

The use of the sea as an airstrip seems such a tempting and simple proposition that you wonder why it is no longer considered an option for global aviation; after all, it was how the first long-haul passenger services were established by Imperial Airways with their fleet of Empire flying boats. On a gin-clear day, when the waters lie flat and unruffled, there seems no better alternative but when the winds rise and the pressure drops, as they are inclined to do along the northwest coast, the ability to take off, and more importantly, to land again and find safe shelter, is at the mercy of the wild, wild sea and horses.

It was inevitable that the presence of RAF and naval bases and the gathering of merchant convoys should attract the attentions of the Luftwaffe. On 23rd December 1940 ships anchored in the Firth of Lorne were attacked by a group of Heinkel He 111 bombers and five suffered damage, among them the SS *Breda*, a Dutch ship which had fled to Britain during the Nazi invasion of the Netherlands. She was part of a convoy destined for Bombay with a rich cargo, which included Tiger Moth biplanes, army lorries, NAAFI supplies, nine dogs and ten horses reputedly belonging to the Aga Khan. In danger of sinking from a flooded engine room, she was towed by tug to calmer waters at Ardmucknish Bay, north of Oban, near Benderloch. The following day, with only a small part of her cargo unloaded, a storm eased her back into deeper waters where she sank and still remains. Some of the horses escaped ashore and some drowned with their boxes as they drifted free from the decks. Over the next four days one horsebox wandered on the tides towards Maiden Island at the entrance to Oban Bay.

The noise inside the flying Sunderlands must have been staggering, reaching a crescendo as the fuselage made contact with the sea; landing these behemoths in the dark seems like a massive leap of faith. In the pitch dark of an Oban winter's night, just after 9pm on 27th December 1940, a young Australian pilot, Ivor Henry Meggitt, was attempting a routine landing in the bay. The noise of the engines and the fuselage riding the sea was interrupted by the almighty sound of metal crashing against metal at high speed – there may be fear in the expected but the really terrifying arises from the sudden and the unexplained. It seems likely that the crew had no idea what had happened as the plane broke up around them in the icy seas just off Maiden Island. The aircraft had hit the wandering horsebox[4] from SS *Breda* with the result that all those aboard were forced to abandon their Sunderland, only one of the eleven crew members managing to survive the freezing conditions.

The Valentine postcard of Ganavan Sands is pre-war and shows the beach when it was a proper seaside destination. There is so much activity. Golfers are walking up the to the first green, bags over their shoulders; there is a campsite just beyond where I imagine the first tee is sited; there is a pavilion, beach huts, swings and roundabouts; there is a boat pulled up on the sands and brave people in the sea; there is the clubhouse and a full car park – the place is alive, pre-dating the advent of package holidays to warmer climes. The golf course was the original 9-hole Oban Golf Club links which opened in April 1890 with a commemorative match between Captain Stewart and Mr Tom Morris of St Andrews. The course is no more but it did at least survive to the end of hostilities, providing loaned equipment and courtesy of the course to the airmen stationed nearby. It is not difficult to imagine the layout, with a deep gulley dissecting the fairways nearest the shore.

Go to Ganavan Sands today and it is a shadow of its former self, every hint of seaside life is gone. Sheep roam the golf course, there is no pavilion, no beach huts, no swings, no roundabouts; all that remains is the slipway and concrete hardstanding where flying boats were once dragged from their watery homes for repairs and maintenance. The only evidence of former glories are inscriptions on the occasional information board and a flying boat silhouette etched into the iron gate that marks the beginning of the National Cycle Network Route 78, a tarmac lane which runs along the edge of the old fairways of Oban Golf Club. This empty scene is overlooked by new-build white apartments which have all the charm and design sensibilities of a PFI-funded hospital complex.

There is another flying boat story. On 23rd August 1942, a Mk III Sunderland flying boat *W4026* left Oban for RAF Evanton following minor repairs. Two days later, following servicing and refuelling, the flying boat ascended from the Cromarty Firth, heading for one of the RAF bases on Iceland. A short time after take-off the crew encountered poor visibility and were forced to fly on instruments. A strong westerly wind drifted the plane off course by a greater margin than the crew had calculated so that the decision to head west for the Pentland Firth was taken too early. The flying-boat flew into the Eagles Rock outcrop above Meall Dhonuill in Caithness and all but one on board perished. The dead included the Duke of Kent, the younger brother of King George VI.

Unless a Royal dies in his bed, it is obligatory that conspiracy theories take hold and this incident is no exception. The joy of the modern world is that no matter how harebrained your theory you will always find someone on the internet who shares your beliefs. It is the joined-up world's strength and its weakness – the font of all knowledge, the font of all lies and everything in between. It is the inside of all our heads. *It is a wonderful feeling when you discover some evidence to support your beliefs* – Anonymous, Forbes.com

Notes

1. The record and film producer, Joe Boyd, recalls *making music in the 1960s* in his memoir, *White Bicycles* – this quote is from the book's prologue.

2. This fragment from a very private life is detailed in James Carron's *The Remarkable Life of James McRory Smith*.

3. This quote is from Don McCullin's harrowing autobiography – *Unreasonable Behaviour* – Chapter 17, Lessons of War.

4. History does not record if the box was empty – I prefer to think it was one that drifted away after the horse was rescued.

Tobermory

Chapter **6**

Your sons and your daughters are beyond your command.
Bob Dylan[1]

As the car ascended the ramp from the ferry at Craignure, the intention had been to head straight for Tobermory. I was heading in the right direction but was then distracted, tempted from the straight and narrow, the story of my life. The subject of my distraction on this occasion was innocent enough, an unprepossessing entrance marked *Craignure Golf Club, Visitors Welcome* – it would seem ill-mannered to pass it by. On this occasion, my compulsive behaviour worked to the good. I missed the local police lurking up the road at Salen with their handheld speed camera, waiting to catch the unsuspecting tourist – *welcome to Mull!*

114

The diminutive clubhouse and greenkeeper's shed sit back from the road, a modest course in a fine setting. The clubhouse may be rough around the edges, but you suspect that more fun is had within these musty walls than in many grander establishments.

Hanging on a wall is a photograph that springs directly from its origins (reproduced by kind permission of Craignure Golf Club); the image shows a doughty lady golfer driving off as a formation of aircraft fill the sky above. They could be Spitfires or Lysanders and it could be a land girl taking some well-earned recreation, but the reality is that they are light planes from the local Glenforsa grass airstrip and the lady is not one of my mother's war time colleagues but Mrs Violet de Klee whose family were responsible for the original course laid out in 1895.

The picture actually dates from 1980 when the course was reopened, having fallen into disuse for a good number of years. The fly-past was organised by David Howitt who owned the Glenforsa Hotel and adjacent airstrip and who played a large part in designing and reviving the course. Like Inveraray, the fairways are a touch too receptive and some areas too closely resemble wetlands, but it sits so close to the shore that it is impossible to resist.

The Craignure scorecard is like an orienteering map and for the casual visitor this presents something of a challenge. The complications arise because there are many more tee boxes than greens. There are no entirely blind holes, but knowing where to go or even where to start from can be a mystery. The first par 4 demands a good drive to clear some particularly soggy ground either side of a ditch that stretches across the course to join the Scallastle River. The second, *Lochlinnhe*, is the highlight – played as a par 3 on the way out and a par 4 on the way back, it is the position of the green that delights. There is no need for bunkers, it is more than adequately protected by rocks on the approach and the sea if you go too long; standing on this exposed green, a glorious panorama unfolds in all directions but it's the sea, the sea that draws the attention.

> *It runneth the earth's wide regions round.*
> *It plays with the clouds, it mocks the sky,*
> *Or like a cradled creature lies.*[2]

On the warm March day I played the course, it lay like the cradled creature of the poem while beneath its calm surface rotted the remains of three cannons, jettisoned by the vessel *Dartmouth* before she sank in a heavy storm in October 1690, evidence that golf in this part of the world can indeed be wild.

Up among the rocks adjacent to the second green there is a variety of tee boxes to choose from as the third heads back towards the Scallastle estuary. I drove long and true down the fourth, pitched neatly into a sloping green and then realised I was playing the fifth green or at least

I think I was, there is much to confuse the uninitiated in this corner of the course. The seventh and eighth offer some respite as both reside on their own stretch of land over a distorted footbridge which takes a winding route across the river, while the ninth returns as a par 4 on the front 9 and a 475-yard par 5 on the way in, a testing finish.

*

Craignure was an enjoyable diversion, a good snap decision. We are the sum of decisions, some our own, some others'. It had been decided, I was going to be a doctor. My parents had ambitions for me, way beyond my academic capabilities and entirely alien to my interests. I had decided in my early teens that I just wanted to race, in the 1960s a guaranteed shortcut to the attentions of the medical profession. The path to my destiny would be as a mechanic, an aspiration deemed too lowly, too far beneath the family's status and therefore wholly discouraged. Lacking direction I drifted and then by some curious circumstance spent forty years in the IT industry; something akin to having a desire to be a pro-golfer and ending up playing professional tiddlywinks; fundamentally it was something I never wanted to do.

I was raised an only child by parents who were only children themselves. My sister, born seven years earlier, had an entirely separate upbringing and nothing in my parents, experience saw the need to bring us together. That sort of age and gender gap between siblings is a recipe for solitude. We lived separate lives, there was no jealousy, nothing one wanted that belonged to the other, just an emotional distance. That distance was only bridged when my mother directed torrents of harsh words at my sister.[3] Words are important and not easy to retract even if the originator is not entirely in control. I had grown accustomed to such invective.

If her Dad was immune from Peg's judgements, all my associates were shifted to the other end of the spectrum and none more so than my choice of girlfriends. My first serious entanglement started at the end of the third week of April 1969 and petered out in the summer of '72. This relationship caused such a stir that I was eventually evicted from home. I was absolutely determined never to return.

My modest qualifications found me in a chemical engineering research lab researching nothing in particular while at weekends I worked as a petrol pump attendant to ensure my financial independence; a very strange place indeed. The garage was run by two cricket bat-wielding lesbians whose smile muscles had been surgically removed. I swapped weekend shifts with a teacher, Brian, who was working for nothing after his hands had been caught in the till and was therefore wholly unreliable. The forecourt was shared with a team of second-hand car salesmen who sold nothing, but compensated for the boredom and their lack of income by stealing reams of Greenshield stamps from the lesbians' side of the business. I met Brian rarely, but when I did he demonstrated a remarkable imagination which he enthusiastically applied to a tapestry of tales involving slips, gully, third man and garage owners of unusual sexual orientation. In a Hitchcockian manner he always warned against knocking on their door after 9pm. The ladies seemed to occupy a disproportionate swathe of his inner landscape.

Then, almost on a whim, I became determined to work with computers, a curious decision for someone so wrapped up in the automotive world. There are decisive moments in all our lives and this was mine, a decision all of my own making with no one else to blame – much like my golf.

It seems obvious, but almost uniquely, it is not only a non-contact sport but the object of our frustration, the ball, is entirely motionless at address; it doesn't come screaming at us over a net whipping top spin, it doesn't swoop and bend towards us, twisted by the side of someone's foot, it is stock still. If we slice, hook or even miss the ball entirely, it is our fault, our lack of concentration, our inability to repeat a much-practised sequence of movements. Once away from the tee and into the semi-rough, the rough or the nearest bush, there is no one else to blame but ourselves; if the lie of the ball is terrible, who put it there?

Professionals will blame the green-keepers, the galleries, the photographers, their caddy, their putting coach, their ex-wife, anyone but themselves, but like us all, they are the sole architects of their downfall. The slice into the trees coming up the last at Augusta, the crucial lipped-out putt at the decisive moment in the round; how do they sleep? After some catastrophe on the near verge of success, I will replay events for days after, but what is the mental condition of someone who has just let the Open slip from his grasp, do they ever completely recover? Scott Adams was four shots ahead of the field on the final day of the 2012 Open, but let the Claret Jug slip from his grasp – *'I know I've let a really great chance slip through my fingers today, but somehow I'll look back and take the positives from it'*. I found it difficult to imagine what those positives might have been. Even though it was the much-admired Ernie Els who benefited from his collapse, the majority, including Ernie, were genuinely saddened by Adams' failure, recognising only too well the disappointment and the angst to come.

There is no concept of sitting on a safe lead, playing for time, three nil up with only five minutes to play; every golf shot counts to the last. In a fine example of natural justice, Scott Adams survived the rigours of Augusta to win the Masters in 2013, sinking a final putt in the play-off with Ángel Cabrera, which I would not have got within 10 feet of the hole – just how many tedious hours of repetitive practice does that kind of skill take? – many more hours than I could possibly imagine, I suspect. As a reward, the victorious at Augusta can sit in that uniquely contrived and dimly awful setting, the Butler Cabin, and thank everyone from God down, but the success is entirely their own and they know it. As in golf, as in life, when chances come they need to be grasped but, not everyone does. The life of the professional golfer seems especially self-centred; there is only one person that matters, I am that person and I must succeed, a team game it is not. Tiger Woods has spent his entire existence in that frame of mind; he is, or was, almost programmed to succeed as a loner, he is no team player. Contrast him with Ian Poulter in the Massacre at Medinah, the 2012 Ryder Cup – elevated to a team player, motivated to succeed for the sake of others and not just himself, he became a man possessed and took the rest of the team with him. The impression is of someone not altogether at ease with the game he has chosen for his career and, just maybe, sometimes he wishes he was walking out at Arsenal's stadium rather than Augusta in April. From the sidelines, this suggests a more rounded human being.

*

The road north to Salen then Tobermory runs very close to the Craignure course, so much so that golfers are warned of its proximity at the ninth tee. This is advice guaranteed to induce a monstrous slice towards the tarmac – if you are passing, ensure your windscreen is insured.

As the road leaves Salen it reduces to a single track and only expands again briefly on the approach to Tobermory, otherwise the island's road system is single track throughout, echoing how all Highland roads were constructed until quite recent times – a road system that travelled over and around the landscape rather than scything a route through it. Forced to a slower pace, the traveller had a far more intimate experience of the Highland geography. In stark contrast, these roads also provide the basis for some hair-raising special stages as the Tour of Mull rally testifies.

Tobermory is the home of the children's TV series, *Balamory*, although this association has completely passed me by. I was raised on *Watch with Mother* while my own offspring moved on to more 'serious' offerings sometime after *Postman Pat* was top of the bill. Fortunately they were all born too early to suffer the speech-impeded *Teletubbies*, creatures whose pointy heads suggest something more practical than their unintelligible utterances; golf ball retrievers perhaps?

Balamory or *Tobermory*, either way the approach down a steep hill into town is like walking into an auditorium, passing between the old bonded warehouse and the distillery as the stage sweeps around the waterfront and the multi-coloured buildings, the pier providing a cat-walk to the sea. Not only is it pretty to look at, this town possesses all the right ingredients: a book and tackle shop combined, post office, bank, chandler, ironmonger, baker, a variety of restaurants including Chinese and Indian, silver and goldsmith, hairdresser, shoe shop, soap maker and supermarket – as with so many out-of-the-way places, where would these Highland towns be without the Co-op. There are sizeable mainland communities with much less variety.

There is also a town clock erected in 1905 on the instruction of Isabella Bird in memory of her sister Henrietta, who died of typhoid in Tober-mory in 1880. Isabella was an adventuress, explorer, writer and the first female fellow of the Royal Geographical Society. She enjoyed ill health, suffering from a range of psychogenic illnesses. When she was doing exactly what she wanted she was almost always as fit as a fiddle much in the way that golfers rarely feel off colour on the golf course. I confess I am not struck by the clock, but I have seen worse. To mark the Millennium, my home town of Hale in Cheshire erected a clock of similar proportions, possibly the ugliest example of urban com-memorative architecture in the country – take a look some time, Stalin would have loved it. Coincidentally, both the Tobermory and Hale clocks are sited adjacent to fountains, the Hale example serving only to accentuate the ugliness of the other. Tobermory, relatively less well-off and remote, escaped the plague of town planners that desecrated so many towns in the 1960s and 1970s. Hale is a fine example, a wealthy suburb of Manchester. With money came egos and with egos came big self-aggrandising ideas. Down came the Council Offices and Drill Hall, up went the supermarket and hotel, planning vandalism of the worse kind. The old railway crossings near the Millennium Clock have been replaced by European-style barriers, so the town now looks for all the world like an East-West border crossing from the Cold War.

In the Gods above the town of Tobermory is the Golf Club. The approach must be the most devious of any course in the land. Turning left at *Tackle and Books*, Back Brae does a sharp left by the Indian restaurant before a right hairpin takes you around the back of the very solid Western Isles Hotel. From there it is a sharp left uphill, a sharp right and an immediate sharp left before turning right onto Erray Road, passing the police station on the left. The course entrance is in a dip a few hundred yards along on the right. There is another less complicated route, but the signs take the unsuspecting visitor this way for reasons that I trust go beyond simple tribal revenge.

Tobermory Golf Club was established in 1896 with support from the local John Hopkins & Co. Whisky Distillers. Starting at Erray before spending a number of years at Sgriobruadh on the road to Glengorm Castle, it is a landscape which seems purpose-built for tee and pins fluttering in a mild westerly. *'Various garden implements were put at the disposal of the club'* while cattle were *'to be grazed on Sunday and Monday only'* – golf, Jim, but not as we know it.

In 1935 The Western Isles Hotel, under the ownership of MacBraynes, purchased land at Erray for the construction of an 18-hole course, and within a short time the Sgriobruadh course was closed and the clubs combined as the Western Isles Golf Club, continuing successfully until the outbreak of war. In 1947 the course reopened with 9 holes due to the maintenance overheads of the full 18 and the ever-present threat of grazing cattle, a problem that would not be finally solved until new fencing was installed in 1973. It would be 1987 before the committee proposed reverting to the original title of the Tobermory Golf Club, and the land was purchased from the owner of the Western Isles Hotel, finally severing the fifty-two-year link with this Victorian establishment. The club has survived a whole series of existential threats and a number of dramatic crises, including the treasurer departing with the club's funds and the police being called to separate the captain and greenkeeper; all par for the course when you have existed for over 110 years. It now seems to thrive.

Par for the course – a strange idiom, usually implying something ordinary, whereas for most golfers, par would be just fine. *Below par* makes even less sense. As I lined myself up for the first, *Ben Hiant*, I am fully expecting to be well *above* par, not least because it is completely blind, not just visually impaired but the whole flying mammal, there really are no clues other than the pole on the horizon. I guess the locals settle for an iron shot to the top of the hill and then play the hole from the plateau where everything, including the hazards, is visible. Unfortunately, I am not that sort of golfer. It is a 356-yard par four so that must be a driver which means that on this hole the ball could be down in a gully, up against a small tree or lost in some rough to the left. At first attempt the ball wedged in a small tree, and I only found it when making the return journey along the eighth. Needless to say, I still used my driver from the first on the back nine. Like I say, I am that sort of golfer – I keep doing the same thing over and over again and expect a different result, the first sign of madness. The course guide suggests that the further right you go, the longer the hole gets – just remove the word 'right'. The reward is not the golf shot, the reward is the view. The Highland landscape unfolds before you – it is like being pinned to the centre of a zoetrope. From the plateau it is a mid-iron to the sweetly placed green; down in the gully it is all 'blind as a bat' again and anyone's guess.

As you leave the first green and climb slightly higher to the second tee it just gets better. To the south are the town and its bay, to the east Calve Island and the mainland, to the north Ben, Hiant, Loch Sunart and Ardnamurchan and to the west Mull's interior and northern coast. Spend some time taking in the landscape because after the testing starter comes the stroke index one, *Creagan,* and you will need your wits about you; the course may be well under five thousand yards (for 18 holes) off the yellows, but it is no pushover. The first shot takes you back to the gully that you crossed from the first, except it is further down the hill with fewer hazards, but then it is a dogleg right up to the second green which is more or less on a level with the plateau from the first; in other words it is a steep climb up to an invisible green. What is it about uphill approaches? Too short and the ball stops dead on the elevation. Too long and with nothing to bar its way, the ball might never be seen again – out of fear I always come up short and, still, it is a difficult chip to the green, especially if the pin is to the front.

A round here can too easily start badly, so the third, *Drimnin*, a long downhill par 3 to a slightly elevated green, comes as light relief. I became fond of this hole because at that sort of distance I can let rip with a driver and on the first two attempts I hit the green – miracles happen.

Drimnin is a small settlement which is visible across a sparkling Sound of Mull when the day is clear of sea mists. There are many remote places in the Highlands and Islands yet despite its relatively southern location and its geographical proximity to Tobermory, Drimnin is one of the more inaccessible places; it really is at the back end of nowhere. It is 12 miles down a single-track road from Lochaline, which itself is hardly the centre of the universe, and from Lochaline it is a further 30 miles to the Corran Ferry where you can begin to think about civilisation at Fort William, another 10 miles north. My wife defines civilisation as anywhere possessing a Marks & Spencer, but, to be fully compliant, it should also include a Waitrose and Zara. On all three counts Fort William doesn't comply unless you include M&S Dental Care Ltd at Glen Nevis Place.

My definition is simpler, to be civilised a place must possess a golf course. Tobermory is tantalisingly close for any golfers at Drimnin but they would have to be keen despite the choice of ferry routes; either by car from Lochaline to Fishnish or a direct passenger ferry from Drimnin jetty to Tobermory pier. How better to arrive for a day's golf?

> *The great seas number seven, and I've sailed them in my day*
> *But there's no place nearer Heaven, than Tobermory Bay*

Angus MacIntyre – verse from *'Conversation at Tobermory Pier'*

At Drimnin jetty there is a cairn in memory of Charles Maclean, killed leading the MacLeans who were supporting the House of Stuart at the Battle of Culloden in 1746. As Killin is home to the McNabs, so Mull is home to the MacLeans. Their ancestral pile, Duart Castle, stands a majestic guard on the approaches to Craignure. In my first year at primary school I vividly remember paying great attention to a history lesson where soldiers moved in swathes across a busy blackboard and a cloud of chalk dust. I was convinced it was the story of my grandfather in the First World War and then promptly lost interest when I realised it all happened in 1066. Since then I have always preferred my history to be more contemporary, something more recent, something I can relate to. While the story of the MacLeans spans the centuries, it is the oblique historical connections which fascinate.

When Samuel Johnson and James Boswell visited in 1773, their host was Sir Allan MacLean, 22nd Chief and head of the Clan Maclean, who took them on a boat trip to Inch Kenneth, a small island situated at the mouth of Loch Na Keal, lying off the western shores of Mull. On the island there are the ruins of a twelfth century chapel which contains funeral monuments and carved stones dating from mediaeval times, not only commemorating the MacLeans but also, it is said, some kings of Scotland, a more accessible resting place when storms prevented passage to Iona. It was within these ancient ruins that the brain-damaged Unity Mitford, thinking herself a clergyman, would conduct imaginary church services and then fly off in a rage when she could not find her words; a scene from the imaginings of Charlotte Brontë. The well-documented six Mitford girls were glamorous, romantic and in their political affiliations, highly controversial, not least Unity and her obsessive friendship with Hitler.

It is the best and the worst place,[4] Inch Kenneth, with its four storeyed, cream-painted house was acquired by their father, David Mitford, in 1939. A nineteenth-century building adapted in the thirties, it is an odd mixture, seemingly a fortified country house with a castellated bow front. David was there with his wife Sydney when war was declared with Germany on 3rd September. In Munich, on the same day, Unity walked to the Englischer Garten, took a small automatic pistol from her handbag, fired one shot in the ground, then put the pistol to her right temple and fired again. Unity could not cope with the divided loyalties certain to arise from the outbreak of hostilities, hostilities that would also divide the staunchly patriotic David and the Nazi-sympathising Sydney. Unity survived, utterly changed.

Conceived in Swastika, Ontario, born on 8th August 1914, days after war was declared, christened Unity Valkyrie and later adopting the German spelling Walküre (war maiden), her fate seems almost inevitable and intended. Offered the chance of German citizenship and residence in Munich or a safe return home, she chose the latter. It was Hitler who arranged her transfer to Berne with a German nurse before her eventual stretchered return to England in January 1940, *'glad to be in England, even if I'm not on your side'* she declared on arrival. Her mother devoted the next eight years of her life to nursing her severely damaged daughter.

Like many areas in the remote northwest during the war, Inch Kenneth was designated a restricted zone and due to their Nazi sympathies, Sydney and Unity were banned from going there until 1944, although they somehow avoided internment. Unity's health then went into further decline, becoming delusional and incontinent so that Sydney had to wash her white bed sheets every morning, hanging them to dry at the front of the house, billowing across the bay as if in surrender. In May 1948 the bullet from her attempted suicide moved inside her head. Always deemed too dangerous to be surgically removed, it resulted in cerebral swelling and, finally, meningitis. Transferred to Oban hospital, she died a few days later. Sydney would die on the same island in 1963, attended by four of her daughters, Nancy, Pamela, Diana and Deborah: not for the first time, a clan gathering on Innis Choinnich for the passing of a chief. The only absentee was the communist Jessica who by this time owned the island and would sell up in 1966 having at one time mischievously suggested it might become a Soviet submarine base. Deborah Mitford (the Dowager Duchess of Devonshire) talking about Inch Kenneth in 2010 said: *'You always have the feeling that you are coming back. I always have the feeling I am coming back even if I know quite well I am not'*.[5] It is the place, it is the light, it is the desire to never let go. It is why we paint. It is why we photograph. It is why we write.

*

The fourth, another par 3, and the fifth, a short par 4, track along the lower reaches of the course and both provide the opportunity to recover a card suffering from that tough start. There is a short climb

127

to the next tee as the course borders the coastal path below. *Sunart*, a 373-yard uphill par 4 to the top of the course plays long – bring out the driver. As with so many golf holes, it is the second shot that really counts and inevitably you will still be some distance from the green; I lost confidence with fairway woods in the dim and distant past so I always resort to a 'rescue' club, a label which should be banned under the 1968 Trades Description Act. By whatever route you get there, the arrival at the sixth green is again rewarded by a panorama of nature at her best: acres of reflected light, lone islands, empty uplands, high mountains and water, water everywhere. I always have the feeling I am coming back.

The seventh short par 3, *Raeric*, is the signature hole. Played across another deep gully, there is out-of-bounds all along the right, while to the back and front of the green are rocks which can launch even a mildly wayward ball into the stratosphere. Landing the ball plumb centre is remarkably satisfying; there is the certain soaring flight of the ball, the slow motion descent and the reassuring thump from a receptive green. That white spot amid the bright green, not too far from the red flag flapping in a mild breeze, is as pretty as any painting. There is the contented walk up and down the gully, a precursor to the possible birdie and an almost certain par; it is for moments like this we turn out.

The eighth is a blind par 4 taking you back across the top of the gully that you traversed on the first and second; in my case it was the opportunity to find that ball I lost from my first drive and take back a dropped shot. A completely different set of rules apply to the lone golfer regardless of what those fastidious enblazered rule makers might devise in the dusty corridors of the Royal and Ancient.

The fairway at the top of the hill and beyond is wide and forgiving, allowing an unhindered downhill approach shot to the right. Nevertheless, a too enthusiastic drive from the tee or badly struck second shot could find some very unforgiving rough in front of the descent to the next level. Kindly, on a dry day, the ground gathers the ball towards the green, although putting over the ridge that runs from left to right can be difficult and rob a certain par. The last hole is deemed the easiest on the course and should present a relaxing finish, but I found this completely misleading. It is short, but there is danger all down the right and I could never bring myself to go anywhere other than well left. This leaves a very short approach shot over a ridge which protects the green along its left-hand side. If the pin is close to the ridge this can make life very difficult, while a thinned shot will fly into that dangerous rough you were trying to avoid from the tee.

To the end, it is a challenging, interesting and spectacular place to play golf. I always have the feeling I am coming back. I *am* coming back.

Notes

1. From the fourth verse of Bob Dylan's classic song, *The times they are a'changin'*. I am uncertain if Dad objected to this "young Communist" on his perceived politics or simply his ideas. *'Your old road is rapidly ageing'* – I certainly took him literally.

2. The first verse from the poem *'The Sea'* by Bryan Waller Procter (pseud. Barry Cornwall: 1787–1874) reproduced in Edmund Clarence Stedman's *A Victorian Anthology* (McCullin, 1990).

3. This is one of the many disturbing symptoms of vascular dementia.

4. Deborah Mitford speaking in the Simon Morris documentary film – *If These Walls Could Speak: Inch Kenneth*, completed in September 2010.

5. Another Deborah Mitford quote from the film *If These Walls Could Speak*.

6

To Traigh

Once, in the wilds of Afghanistan,
I lost my corkscrew and we were
forced to live off nothing but food
and water for days. W. C. Fields[1]

The small eight car ferry takes you the 4.5 nautical miles from Tobermory to Kilchoan on the southern coast of the Ardnamurchan peninsula. It is not Afghanistan but you would be well advised to keep hold of your corkscrew.

Caledonian MacBrayne monopolise water-borne transport on the west coast, but the overly administered twenty-first century does have its compensations. Despite their monopoly, the fares are reasonable and their boats comfortable if not luxurious. This was not always the case; they were once described as scarcely an advance on the emigrant ships of the nineteenth century clearances. *'Indeed MacBrayne's were too often in the same line of business and operating at about the same level of concern'* – Alasdair Maclean, *Night Falls on Ardnamurchan.*

It is a civilised crossing, but this has not always been the case and our rose-tinted view of the past can be more than just a colour distortion. M. E. M. Donaldson writing in the 1920s describes a trip on a MacBrayne boat as a *'floating slum ... what shelter there was available was amongst the cattle and the cargo in the unsavoury hold ... MacBrayne exercise what amounts practically to a despotic monarchy in the Western Highlands, and treat the public as they please, without let or hindrance. They charge one shilling carriage for a single joint of beef on the half hour crossing from Tobermory to Kilchoan. Compare, too, the freight of thirty shillings per ton charged from Bombay to Glasgow, a thirty days' voyage.'* [2] Such was MacBrayne's infamy that Highland mothers once taught their children this rhyme:

The earth unto the Lord belongs
With all that it contains,
Except, of course, for the Western Highlands
And that's owned by MacBrayne's

When did a more comfortable age begin, at what point in history did the coloured lights get turned on after the austere post-war years? It was gradual but there seems to have been a turning point, a point when an older, gentler-paced world tilted towards a younger, faster, more violent one. Perhaps it was the year that the Boeing 747 made its maiden flight and the Harrier Jump Jet entered service, the same year the first ATM appeared. The year that Judy Garland died and De Gaulle stepped down. The year that Gaddafi came to power, the year of Manson, Sharon Tate, Helter Skelter and British troops being deployed in Northern Ireland. The year of Led Zeppelin 1, Abbey Road and the Apollo 11 and 12 moon landings. Perhaps it was 1969, the year Jacklin won the Open, the year the boy from Dumbuck Garage first became World Champion and my 1960s began.

The year my adult life began did not start well, but it could all have been so much worse. That crowded 1968 Christmas my sister brought another of her suspect boyfriends home to stay over the holiday period; nothing personal, all her boyfriends at that age were suspect. This one was different again; for one thing, I think he was married, although that inconvenient truth only emerged much later. Nevertheless, Mum's antenna was switched on and with little room at the inn, I was sleeping in my parents' bedroom. I was parked on a camp bed at the bottom of their bed – I was woken by *'Ken, Ken, Ken – I am sure of it, I have seen that man on Police Five'*. If she had already seen him walking up the aisle it would have been a more accurate premonition.

I soon warmed to the innocent boyfriend. A professional squash player, he owned a trendy new Viva GT with Rostyle wheels and a matt black bonnet, all the rage at the time. He was so keen to win approval, or more likely just a decent bloke, he offered to loan me his car to drive down to Mallory Park Race Circuit on Boxing Day, but my parents declined his generosity on my behalf. Without this intervention I would have happily stuffed his car across the Derby Ring Road roundabout rather than my own precious Mini. Here is the odd thing. He had a good friend who had *'decided to become Formula 1 racing driver'*. My good friend William and I smiled politely and laughed heartily out of earshot.

Nobody can just *decide to become a Formula 1 racing driver*, particularly one we had never heard of at any level of the sport. In our minds, it was slightly more ambitious than deciding to become an astronaut and take off to Mars – less skill required, you see. As though fate were out to teach two cynical teenagers a lesson, within five years he was competing in Grand Prix and within eight years he was World Champion – his name, James Hunt. Today I am not sure which I find more surprising; the fact that he reached the pinnacle of motor sport or that there is now a major film of his championship tussle with a damaged Niki Lauda – *Rush,* directed by Ron Howard.[3]

*

The ferry to Kilchoan is at the end of the waterfront next to Café Fish, a great restaurant ideally placed for the catch of the day. You leave the bustling town of Tobermory and then arrive at Kilchoan slipway where there is nothing, except perhaps cars waiting for the return ferry. You have arrived at an entirely different place, you have arrived at the Ardnamurchan peninsula. As you drive up Pier Road to the village, you realise there is more to this place, but not much. At the B8007 it is a left turn towards another Salen, but then I was distracted, again.

Some years ago I read Alasdair Maclean's *Night Falls on Ardnamurchan,* a touching account of the life and death of a crofting community interspersed with extracts from his father's journal; you cannot read this book and not long to go. Suddenly it was there, just a 6-mile unplanned detour to the westernmost point of the British mainland across the old roads which leave no scars as they rise and fall with the undulating landscape.

Sanna announces itself with a cinerama wide open space, sand dunes, distant mountains and huge, huge clouds, as though Wilhelm Reich[4] finally succeeded. There is no discernible end to the north and west horizons, the skies, the seas, the mountains stretch to eternity and this wild place seems near empty.

When I was a child in Sanna I loved best to lie on my back in the summer hayfield where I could be a secret of the grass, where I could stare at the sky watching the clouds form and re-form over Ardnamurchan
Alasdair Maclean

Sanna consists of dunes, rocks, a road that peters to a track, the sound of seabirds, the sea, occasional crofts and homesteads, some abandoned. A map at the beginning of Maclean's book allows the curious to place the family house in the landscape, although not with any degree of precision. Maclean and his father's journal describe an everyday life based on hard toil and the practicalities of survival in an isolated community; now I suspect that the majority come here simply to escape everyday life. Some appear to have made their money and are investing in property while others of a more bohemian nature have settled to scratch out a life at this wild frontier – beyond compare in the heat of the sun, less so in the depths of winter.

Over the road from the Sanna Crofts there is a corrugated iron shed and on one end, in white lettering on a red background, is the message – *Resist UK Entanglement in USA Wars*. Next door and near the Maclean house there is a white stone cottage with bright yellow doors and windows. Strung to the fence is a white sheet which bears a poem on a similar topic, neatly hand written in red and white inks. With so few passers-by there is a sense that he or she or they are preaching to an empty chapel, so here it is for wider consumption:

RAF Waddington Murder Inc
Grim Reaper Drones
Smash Flesh and Bones
In Oil-Rich Lands Far Away
Guided by Geeks – Computer Freaks
Assassins
Killing by Remote Control

I am not certain that Maclean's father, who saw service in the Dardanelles in the First World War and died in 1973, would have been able to begin to imagine the meaning of this message; we forget how much we have 'advanced' these last forty years. Perhaps the desire to escape is understandable and out here on this remote peninsula seems as good as anywhere on this lonely planet.

Driving back to Kilchoan the road heads north and inland to Loch Mudie where brief glimpses of the mountains of Skye fade in and out of the northern view before the road descends again to hug the coast and Loch Sunart. Each lonely outpost along the way is marked by flocks of wandering sheep, a white farmhouse and cattle grids at their borders. Everywhere seems so far from somewhere that you would fear being taken ill in the night.

The road along Loch Sunart winds with the landscape. Climbing out-crops then dropping back to the shore to repeatedly fill the lungs with salt air, it is a spectacular snail's pace drive. In 1847 travellers on this lonely road would have been witness to the arrival of the Floating Church. Built on the Clyde, this two-storey 78-foot-long craft was towed along the Loch to safe anchorage near Strontian where it served the local community until 1870. The need for such a floating com-munion arose in 1843, the year the Christian community of Scotland fractured with the formation of the Free Church of Scotland and the subsequent refusal by the local landowner to allow construction of a Free Church on his estate. Unable to build on land, the congregation raised £1,400 to worship upon the sea.

Men speak of it as a stirring scene, when ropes and cables were run out from the beach and the boats were rapidly passed backwards and forwards conveying the worshippers.
– Annals of the Disruption in 1843, Reverend Thomas Brown

The Floating Church has parallels with the fictional floating glass church of Peter Carey's *Oscar and Lucinda*. Lucinda bets Oscar that he cannot transport a glass church from Sydney to a remote settle-ment 250 miles up the New South Wales coast. The real and the fictional floating churches would both founder, but the glass in Oscar and Lucinda's edifice would have shone more brightly if strontium were added during the manufacturing process.

In the eighteenth century, up to six hundred men were employed in the extraction of lead, silver and zinc at Strontian in the upper reaches of Loch Sunart. In 1790, the mines revealed an entirely new element which would become known as strontium after the village where it was discovered. Despite its late discovery, it is the fifteenth most common element in the Earth's crust and has since been used for a wide variety of applications including toothpaste, fireworks, fluorescent lights, anti-corrosion paint, 3D holographic displays and glass manufacture. It also plays a significant part in improving the cast aluminium process, making it suitable for items that had been traditionally made from iron or steel, most notably lightweight racing engines.

The Cosworth DFV (Dual Four Valve) V8 is the most iconic and successful racing engine in motor sport history, winning on its 1967 maiden outing at Zandvoort in the hands of Jim Clark, it just kept on winning until 1983, clocking its 155th and final victory at the Detroit GP on 5th June. The V8 crankcase, pistons and cylinder head are all cast in aluminium. It is the engine which delivered Jackie Stewart's first World Championship in 1969, Jochen Rindt's posthumous crown in 1970 and Stewart's second the following year. As early as 1971, books were being written about this automotive masterpiece – the heroically named *Such Sweet Thunder*.

What is the attraction of an autograph and why do we collect them? Maybe it represents a unique physical manifestation of the individual. When all else is gone, the mark on the page is tangible evidence that the person once passed close by. There are photographs and there are words but they lack the same direct personal interaction; there are intervening processes which put the subject at a distance.

My first autograph was Jimmy Adamson's: player, coach and manager at Burnley FC. Just a scrap of paper signed in his playing days when he visited my school in 1963. Long since lost, that was the extent of my 'collection' until I started haunting Formula 1 paddocks in the late 1960s and early '70s.

In order to preserve these marks upon a page I took to getting books signed, ideally those with some relevance to the subject. On the afternoon of 23rd October 1971 I bought *Such Sweet Thunder: The Story of the Ford Cosworth DFV Grand Prix Engine*. I then wandered around the Brands Hatch paddock on the eve of the Victory Race, held to celebrate Stewart's second world title. The autographs belong to Stewart, Ronnie Peterson (died from injuries sustained at the Italian GP, 1978) and Jo 'Seppi' Siffert with a photo I snatched just before he signed the book.

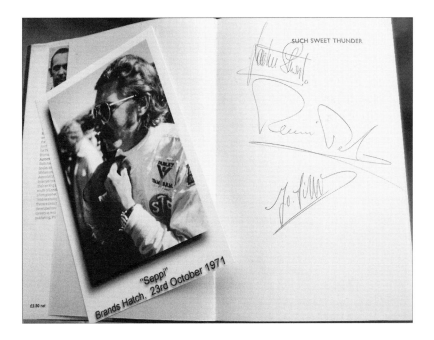

I was there for his best of days in 1968 and his worst of days in 1971. The next afternoon Seppi was gone, a suspension failure threw the car off the track at Hawthorns, the fuel tank ruptured and the black smoke rose again behind Druids from where we could see the rest of the field slowly peeling off into the pit lane. A celebration had turned into a wake under a 9/11 sky and I never asked for an autograph again.

*

Through Glenmore with its Nadurra Visitor Centre, Glenborrodale with its castle and wholly inappropriate fencing, keeping them in or us out, it is not clear which, finally you arrive at Salen where the road to Arisaig heads north and west from the left turn at the junction with the A681. Through Acharacle, Dail Nam Breac, Kinlochmoidart, Glenuig and finally Roshven, this stunning drive eventually emerges onto the A830 Fort William to Mallaig road. A broad modern highway it is immediately evident that its direct route owes more to dynamite than hand and shovel. Complete with Armco and crawler lanes, the road scythes through hillsides and the traveller is removed from the immediacy of the landscape.

Perhaps we should be grateful; Batsford and Fry writing in the early 1930s described a road that '*twists and dips along its course is probably without exception the worst – or at least the worst in Scotland – medieval in its surface as in its writhings'*.[5]

Fortunately it is only eight miles until the Arisaig turn-off and the road to Traigh where the passing places return and we head back to the coast and a very special golf course.

Notes

1. The quotes is from *My Little Chickadee*, a film comedy starring Mae West and W. C. Fields, first released in 1940. Fields famously walked off the set before filming was complete so at least one third was shot with a double.

2. This quote from Mary Ethel Muir Donaldson appears in Alasdair Maclean's *Night Falls on Ardnamurchan* – it is an extract from her book *Further Wanderings Mainly in Argyll*.

3. The film adjusts history for dramatic effect, choosing to start Lauda's F1 career at the 1973 US GP; in reality he had been driving F1 cars for some time prior to this. There is a photograph of Lauda on the www.golfinthewild.co.uk blog; it dates from the British Grand Prix of 1972 and is how I prefer to remember him – a young man still finding his way.

4. Wilhelm Reich was an Austrian psychoanalyst who invented the 'cloudbuster'.

5. From the 1933 travel guide *The Face of Scotland* by Harry Batsford and Charles Fry.

7

Traigh

Whoever you are, I have always depended on the kindness of strangers. Tennessee Williams *– A Streetcar Named Desire*[1]

I t is the kindness of strangers that is the most uplifting and purest form of altruism. It is this that allows us to take solace from tragic events, stories of the unconditional kindness of strangers that emerged after 9/11 and 7/7 counteract our despair. There is also a nagging doubt: would we, in the same circumstance, be capable of the same unconditional compassion? Traigh was once home to a large community of strangers brought together by the special needs of conflict. It was here that some of the bravest men and women of the Second World War learned their craft: *strangers in a strange land.*[2]

Arisaig village is on the B-road that hugs the coastline all the way to Morar, leaving the new A-road to scythe its way towards Mallaig. The golf course at Traigh is about two and a half miles north of Arisaig beyond the oddly named Back of Keppoch, through Bunacaim to Portnaluchaig. The course sits on the very edge of the shore, a few feet back from a roadside livestock fence. A neat, white, rain-washed but 'n' ben-style clubhouse announces your arrival.

A saltire on the flagpole to its southern side provides early warning of the prevailing winds. On a blessèd day the flag will hang limp, the tide will be out revealing golden sand and the sea will reflect a clear blue sky; this will only happen if you are a good person. I am not a good person but the recording angel was not paying close attention the day I arrived; it was just perfect.

Traigh means 'beach' in Gaelic, but there are few sand bunkers on the course unless you stray across the road; the course protects itself quite well enough with plenty of mature gorse. If you drive into the prickly stuff, your ball may be visible but it is probably best left where it lies unless you want to be unpicking gorse needles from your clothing for the next few months.

There has been a golf course at Traigh since the turn of the last century. Owned by the local estate, it was originally established for the sole use of the owners and their guests. Not far south, inland from Back of Keppoch, there was a members' club which was used until 1939 and then abandoned during the war; it was never reopened and now lies hidden beneath the by-pass. In 1945, Traigh House was acquired by the current owner's mother and the course immediately made available to local golfers.

The original private Traigh course occupied about 35 acres with nine intertwined fairways squeezed within its limited confines; it was an

integral part of the farm and used for evening grazing of sheep and cows. Between 1992 and 1995 the course was enlarged to 50 acres by adding land to the rear of the large dunes that originally marked its eastern boundary. This additional stretch of peat land has provided room for the appropriately named Lang Whang par 5. This new challenging layout was designed by the golf architect, John Salvesen with help from the Head Greenkeeper at Royal Lytham St Annes, James MacDonald, a native of Arisaig. John Salvesen, who died in 2008, was responsible for designing courses at Charlton and Elmwood in Fife, the Strathmore at Alyth, and a new course in southern Norway, but he was always most proud of his work at Traigh; none of the others could match this spectacular setting.

The course belongs to the owner of Traigh House and while the club aims to be self-financing, occasional cash injections are required to help balance the books. Lean times inevitably strike such small enterprises, which are dependent in equal measure on two highly unpredictable variables: visitors and favourable weather. Traigh House is visible at the northern end of the course beyond the sixth green and it has history.

In 2002 the owner, Mr Jack Shaw-Stewart, hosted a small ceremony to unveil a plaque in honour of the Second World War Special Operations Executive's (SOE) Special Training Schools (STS) based in the Arisaig and Morar area from 1941. The plaque commemorates Special Forces from the Army of Czechoslovakia who received training at Traigh House prior to returning home and undertaking operations against the Nazi occupiers. The unveiling was performed by Major-General Antonin Petrak, an extraordinary man who lived an extraordinary life. An officer in the 39th Infantry Regiment (Bratislava) when the Germans entered Prague in March 1939, he fled to the west. Travelling overland to Syria and then by sea to Marseilles, he joined the Czechoslovak forces stationed at Agde. When France fell he made for England and the Czechoslovak Brigade at Cholmondeley Park, near Chester. He subsequently volunteered to join the SOE and, after an initial six-week course, became the only Czechoslovak instructor at an SOE School based at Traigh House. It is odd to think that on the heavenly quiet sands below the golf course, the SOE trainees would practise beach landings under heavy fire and receive small arms training from Gavin Maxwell (*Ring of Bright Water*).

On 27th May 1942 Operation Anthropoid sought to eliminate the Nazi Reinhard Heydrich, Reichsprotektor of Bohemia, the Butcher of Prague, a high-ranking German Nazi official during the Second World War and one of the main architects of the Holocaust; Petrak was directly responsible for training the assassins at Traigh, Jozef Gabčík and Jan Kubiš. In May 1943, Petrak left the SOE STS to join the 1st Independent Czechoslovak Brigade and take part in the D-Day landings. In command of a company that destroyed German supply dumps around Dunkirk, he was awarded the Military Cross. When he returned home at the end of the war his western allegiances would give rise to brutal treatment under the communist regime and see him serve two prison sentences and considerable time in a forced labour camp.

His eventual rehabilitation was not achieved until the 1989 Velvet Revolution when he was reinstated to the rank of major-general. A holder of the Military Cross, MBE, Order of the White Lion and the Legion d'Honneur, this remarkable man returned to breathe again the free air of Traigh and unveil a perpetual memorial to those who trained and were taught in the SOE's Czechoslovak Section in the Arisaig and Morar area.

In the centre of Arisaig there is a larger granite memorial in the form of an unfolding parachute. Unveiled on 11th November 2009, it also commemorates Czech SOE agents who were dropped behind enemy lines for sabotage operations, inevitably sustaining heavy casualties. The foundation stone of the memorial was blessed by the Holy Father, Pope Benedict XVI – ironically, a conscripted member of the Hitler Youth, the anti-aircraft corps, Luftwaffenhelfer (air force child soldier) and, finally, the German infantry.

The SOE was formed in 1941 when Britain was fighting alone and in no position to mount an invasion force. Churchill's objective was to *set Europe ablaze* through sabotage, assassination and general mayhem across all the occupied countries. This was achieved by using SOE agents to organise, coordinate and arm local resistance groups, not least in France where over four hundred volunteers were parachuted in, thirty-nine of them women, the most famous being 'White Mouse', Nancy Wake, the inspiration for Sebastian Faulks' *Charlotte Gray*. We owe our freedom to these courageous strangers.

Arisaig and Morar were ideally located for this highly secret endeavour, with good rail links despite the remote location and the perfect, empty landscape for the physical fitness, arms, explosives, sabotage and survival technique training that all volunteers undertook during their four-week course. The area was also easily sealed off by the military and locals were issued with passes to enable access to and from their own homes.

On completion of their course in Arisaig, volunteers were transferred to Ringway in Cheshire to complete parachute training, not far from where I was raised; I frequently rode my bike around the decoy landing strips in the shadow of the Jolly Romper pub and the Fairey hangars where the training was completed. In the days of alphanumeric phone numbers, ours was RIN (Ringway) 2171, the phone my sister had glued to her right ear throughout her teenage years. I remember the lone white control tower, the shale car park and the arrival of the first BOAC Bristol Britannia; an internal and external landscape now overwhelmed by the sprawling Manchester Airport. I once organised an EU meeting at one of the airport hotels and proudly took the German delegation for a drink at the Jolly Romper – a pub whose walls were festooned with pictures of Spitfires and Lancaster bombers.

*

As I wander around Traigh golf course looking for an honesty box, two Phantoms explode the silence overhead and disappear south in the blinking of an eye. Higher still, passenger jets scar a clear blue sky with vapour trails. There is no escaping the modern world; there should be no forgetting the past. Eventually, a friendly local turned up to take my green fees and open up the clubhouse – I could proceed to the first tee with a clear conscience, at least in matters related to green fees.

> *'Good sky you've got here McIntyre, well done ... I like this place, the air is good, clear'. Local Hero*, 1983

145

The first par 3, *Captain's Caper*, is a 130-yard steep uphill shot to a partially obscured green – the safe route is to head slightly right to ensure you do not come up short in the rough on the hillside, particularly as the ball tends to gather left once on the green. As you climb the sharp rise from the first tee, it is worth taking a few seconds to draw breath and then turn around to view one of the greatest panoramas of any golf course on Earth with Eigg, Muck and Rhum providing the perfect backdrop. You are playing golf in paradise.

Running across the centre of the course are two high ridges, the gap between the two allowing vehicular access to the greenkeeper's shed and seventh and eighth fairways on the eastern side. The second tee, another *Spion Kop*, is a 70-yard walk to the end of the first ridge. Stand on the tee and wonder at God's architecture: the islands, the white sands and, nestling inland at the end of the course, Traigh House.

This is the course's first of two par 5s, which is shown on the scorecard as a dogleg right towards the third green at the bottom of the hill, near the road. This would appear to be the 'safe' route but a 170-yard drive to the top of the second ridge offers a shorter alternative, only don't drift right; all along the back of the ridge is thick gorse which swallows balls like a whale swallows plankton. I tried this route on my back nine and safely negotiated the gap and then took a straight rescue club for my second; self-satisfied with my bold endeavours, I walked along the ridge to where I had seen my ball land softly and bounce gently left, never to be seen again, it was buried somewhere in the sloping rough. The conventional route offers an uphill iron and then a chip to a punchbowl green surrounded on all sides but one by gorse; there are steps down to the hallowed turf. *Spion Kop* is a rewarding hole to get right and an expensive hole to get wrong.

The tees front and back are the same but the names of the hole are in English from one to nine and in Gaelic from ten to eighteen. I can cope with French pronunciation, I can guess at most German, but to an uneducated Sassenach, Gaelic might as well use the Greek alphabet. The third, *Road to the Isles* or *Rathad nan Eilean*, takes you back down the hill to an inviting green adjacent to the road; 173 yards downhill, there is always the nagging concern that you might over hit onto the road and an innocent passing motorist – campervans are legitimate targets.

The fourth, *Jimmy's Choice*, takes you back up the hill, parallel to the third. With a large tidal burn close by and a green protected by gorse bushes left and right, this is a bit of a devil; it was at this hole that I discovered how well gorse needles embed themselves in a yeti fleece. It is a relatively short par 4 so, if you can drive straight, you should be left with a safe pitch over the magnetic gorse to a two-tiered green; I say 'should' warily.

A short walk back down the hill takes you to the fifth tee and a 125-yard par 3 over the wide tidal burn, *The Bridge* or *Alt an Asaidh*.

I have a sneaking suspicion that I have just written a Gaelic expletive aimed at unsuspecting foreigners. The green is at the northern extremity of the course with a receptive green that slopes towards the tee so that holding the ball on the green should be relatively easy, even for those of us to whom the art of backspin is a complete mystery. The sixth tee is behind the green and the par 4 tee shot takes you back over the burn towards the gorse that threatened on the fourth. The approach to the *McEachen's Leap* green is similar, being protected by gorse left and right and both are blind shots, fine for locals but a mystery for the unbaptised visitor. If you can survive this top corner on a first visit then despite the SI 1 par 5 that follows, your card should be worth keeping.

The seventh, the second par 5, *The Lang Whang (Strac Fada)* heads southwest for 446 yellow yards down the back of the course, all the way to the greenkeeper's shed and the gap between the two main ridges. There is out-of-bounds to the left and a mass of gorse down the right, but the fairway is reasonably generous. On the benign day I played, it seemed relatively straightforward and much easier than the fourth and sixth, but I guess when the wind gusts, a drive into the prevailing south-westerlies could be a much more challenging proposition. Even without a wind I have a tendency to drift right, the professionals call it a fade, I call it a slice. On this occasion it was quite rewarding; a group of solemn, unfriendly visitors had been donating packets of balls to the gorse from the second tee. It was like the Rough Bird had been on an egg-laying spree so I went collecting.

The eighth is another challenging uphill dogleg right par 4, *Local Hero*; David Puttnam was never going to go with the less-than-succinct Gaelic equivalent – *Gaisgeach Ionadail*. The 1983 film stands the test of time; an ageing Burt Lancaster still has the presence of a Hollywood screen legend, but the real star is Camusdarach Beach, just over a mile up the coast from Traigh. It is an oft-told tale that *Local*

Hero was filmed at two entirely different locations, the beach scenes at Camusdarach and the village scenes at Pennan in Aberdeenshire, 185 miles away. Watching the film again, this disregard for geography mildly irritates; there are geological explanations why the landscapes don't match but the real giveaway is the weather. The Camusdarach beach scenes are filmed in glorious Highland and Island reflected light while the village scenes on the 'same day', are filmed in that drab granite light peculiar to the northeast. Fortunately, I am playing golf in weather identical to the former. Perhaps inspired by the light, I drive to the bottom of the hill and then hit a blind seven iron into an uncharted green. As I crest the hill, to my delight, the ball is a secure foot from the pin and a certain birdie for a newly baptised Local Hero; ignorance is bliss.

The last, *Traigh Mhor*, is a glorious, elevated par 3 tee facing once more out to Eigg, Muck and Rhum. In the summer months there is a passenger ferry from Arisaig to these distant islands and the iconic profile of An Sgùrr on Eigg, a profile which keeps changing the closer you get. These are beautiful, distant places but there is no sense of isolation, you are struck not by the distance from the mainland but the cosy proximity of the other islands; you feel as though you are among some tropical archipelago, at least on days when the predominant colour of sea and sky is blue. There are also hints of modernity with some examples of eco-architecture and 24x7 shopping facilities – The Green Shed on Muck sells a range of handmade gifts and achieves round-the-clock service by never locking the door and operating an honesty box with plenty of change. It says much that they not only trust their own but also the visitors; it seems unlikely that the crime rate is high on this or any of the other small islands.

By the ninth I had caught up with a local four ball; three men and a large white mongrel, lying patiently to the side of the green. I would meet them in the small clubhouse later and discuss the round; all four of them were friendly and talkative. The 170-yard drive down to the sloping green is the icing on a very rich cake, just don't drop the crockery; the out-of-bounds field to the left is all too accessible. I am not sure which is worse, a ball buried out of sight in impenetrable rough or, as on this occasion, one sitting proud on sheep-shorn grass, your incompetence all too visible and taunting for the world to see.

My first holiday romance was at a farmhouse near St David's in south Wales. I fell for the farmer's daughter, she was about sixteen and I was barely four. I can still feel her soft hands on my shoulders. She was the first of the gender to make me realise that girls could be loving creatures, unlike my sister, too engrossed in her own older world and my mother, too much in charge. The night the holiday ended, back home, I was distraught, crying a river into Robin-starched sheets. Ever since I have had an overly-moist sentimental streak for people and places left behind. Traigh is such a place.

Notes

1. Tennessee Williams – *A Streetcar Named Desire*: Blanche Dubois has been committed to a mental institution and utters this signature line to the kindly doctor who leads her away.

2. A minor adaptation of *Stranger in a Strange Land*, a 1961 satirical science fiction novel by American author Robert A. Heinlein.

Isle of Skye

Tell me, how does God choose?
Whose prayers does he refuse?
Tom Waits – *Day After Tomorrow*[1]

The road north from the golf course meanders along the coast tracing a path once occupied by a series of SOE Special Training Schools, each designated a unique alphanumeric identifier; there is Traigh House, SOE STS 25c and on the right before the road cuts between Garramor and Camusdarach, SOE STS 25a and 25b respectively. This small stretch of coastline has hidden history and some of the best golden-sanded beaches in Europe; the sun just needs to be shining to see them at their best. The road slips behind Beinn an Achaidh Mhor before eventually rejoining the incongruous main road just south of Morar. Heading north towards Mallaig, there is much to be said for taking an immediate right, picking up the old road into the village and crossing the River Morar in the shadow of the railway viaduct. The river connects Loch Morar with the sea where close to its solitary banks sit STS 22 – Rhubana Lodge, STS 23 – Meoble Lodge and STS 23b – Swordland; a place too beautiful to learn the arts of death and destruction.

The railway keeps close company up to the village before a level crossing takes you back to its west side, passing the too-obvious Morar Hotel and returning to the A-road north to Mallaig.

Just over a mile further north, the old high road can be picked up again by turning right at the junction signposted Glasnacardoch. This road climbs across and above the railway line providing an uninterrupted view of the islands from up in the gods. It passes the surprisingly named *Gordon Brown Place*, the recently built Mallaig High School, the church, shops and hotels before descending Annies Brae and then

Davies Brae into Mallaig's harbour and centre; a much more satisfying route than the tradesman's entrance taken by the lower road which arrives unannounced at the ferry terminal.

From Mallaig it is over the sea to Skye, the best and traditional way to travel to the isle. As the ferry heads north to Armadale, the Knoydart peninsula fills the eastern horizon, home to the most northerly Special Training Schools, STS 24b at Glaschoille and STS 24a at Inverie House. The village of Inverie is as remote as you can get on mainland Britain; it is home to the remotest pub, the Old Forge, a small but thriving community and 7 miles of road which leads precisely nowhere. The only way in and out is by foot or ferry; a 20-mile hike across the Rough Bounds or a 45-minute ferry from Mallaig.

Before and after the war, Inverie House was owned by Lord Brocket, a Nazi sympathiser who, in the company of Unity Mitford, attended Hitler's fiftieth birthday celebrations. Brocket must have been intensely irritated when the house was requisitioned for use as an SOE STS, although given his background, it is certain he was not made aware of its precise role. The story is that, when the family returned to the house after the war, anything that might have been tainted by service personnel was dumped in Loch Nevis; this included everything from the kitchens, bathrooms and toilets. At the bottom of the Loch lie knives, forks, spoons and toilet seats, evidence, if it were needed, that there is no direct correlation between privilege and intelligence.

Nancy Wake was one of the more famous temporary residents at Inverie House. Born in New Zealand, she was living in Marseille and married to a Frenchman, Henri Fiocca, when the Germans invaded France. Nancy immediately became active in the Resistance and by 1943 the Gestapo were hell-bent on catching the elusive White Mouse eventually prompting a perilous escape via Spain, which was only successful at the sixth attempt. Once in Britain, she joined the ranks of the SOE, undergoing training at the 'madhouse' (Inverie) before parachuting back into France to coordinate the Resistance preparations for the Allied landings. During those war years her life was a constant exposure to life-threatening risk and decisions and yet she survived the war and lived into her nineties. *How does God choose, whose prayer does he refuse?*

*

When someone died in our street the curtains were drawn and I was made to stay in indoors; forbidden to play outside, I moped, resentful at the inconvenience. Stranger still, Mum draped a sheet over the dressing table mirror in my sister's bedroom at the front of the house, a superstition based on a passing soul being captured by the silvered, reflective surface. I doubt she had much truck with such beliefs but she worried eternally about the neighbours' opinions, in this world and possibly the next. There was no peeping from the curtains to see the coffin slide into the hearse, there was no making a noise, just a peculiar, never-ending day which was invariably bright and sunny.

These ritualistic social displays have all but disappeared; death has become a taboo subject, *'banished to the private space of the hospital'*.[2] Against all the evidence, twenty-first century man has an almost child like belief in his immortality. But for the incompetence of NHS consultants/doctors/nurses (delete as appropriate) dearest mother/ father/grandfather/grandmother would still be with us, a healthy 120 year old. Accidents do not happen, only human failings which can be fixed by enquiries, bureaucracy, procedure and box ticking. A letter to the *Telegraph* in 2013 about Britain's new growth industry, public inquiries, encapsulated the situation neatly: *'The same tired old platitudes: "Lessons have been learnt", "Things must change", "This must never be allowed to happen again", but they aren't, they don't and it is'.* It was not always like this – on Saturday afternoon on lap 35 of the 1955 Le Mans 24 hours Pierre Levegh's Mercedes 300 SLR clipped the rear of Lance Macklin's Austin Healey 100, veered left and launched into the crowd. Levegh and 83 spectators were killed and a further 120 injured; the race continued to its conclusion at 4pm the following day. Somewhere between these extremes a balance needs to be struck; perhaps a public inquiry is required.

In the summer of 1970, Jochen Rindt, in his second year with Chapman, was progressing inexorably towards the World Championship in the Lotus 72; somehow it seemed inevitable. Motor racing is, or at least was, not about nationality. Where the drivers came from was of no consequence, where the cars were made irrelevant; they were all gods. The distinguishing factor was simply talent; just who was considered the fastest, the most entertaining, *the* driver who could be relied upon to give his all in the pursuit of glory. At any one time there were maybe three or four who stood apart from the rest and Rindt was definitely among them. He was always entertaining to watch and, to use James Hunt's apt description, you could tell he was trying from the *'body language'* of the car; it was all so much more obvious in the days before aerodynamics took hold.

At the 1969 Montjuïc Park Spanish GP, Barcelona, Rindt had suffered an almighty crash when the high wing support on his Lotus 49 had collapsed, the aerofoil lifted and he became airborne. Photographs from the incident show a track littered with debris, not just from Rindt's car but also Hill's identical Lotus which had suffered the same failure just a few laps earlier. When he arrived at the French GP two months later he was still suffering from the consequences of this accident in Spain. In 1969 the French event was held at Clermont Ferrand high in the Auvergne mountains. The track has 51 corners per lap with an altitude difference of over 500 feet which, combined with the intense heat of the cockpit and a full face helmet, conspired to give Jochen motion sickness; during practice he had to stop every two laps to be ill. It was not until Piers Courage loaned him his old open face helmet that he was able to clock some respectable lap times. Although the following venues were quite different from Clermont Ferrand he would not overcome his aversion to the full face helmet until almost a year later at the Belgian Grand Prix, but by then he had instead decided against wearing the crotch strap on his racing harness, believing that this might trap him in a burning car.

The Monza circuit of the 1970 Italian GP was a quite different track from the sanitised modern-day version; with no chicanes it was all about straight-line speed and slipstreaming. To gain maximum advantage the cars ran without wings and this seemed to destabilise the Lotus 72 more than most. On Saturday 5th September during practice, his car veered left under braking, driving into the Armco barriers at racing speed as he approached the last corner before the start/finish line, Parabolica. Without his crotch strap, Jochen slid down in the cockpit and suffered unsurvivable throat injuries caused by the seat-belt buckle. On the Monday after his Montjuich accident on the edge of sleep he had mumbled to his wife Nina: *'I always wondered what Jimmy felt at Hockenheim. Now I think I know: nothing'*. He subsequently became the sport's first and only posthumous F1 world champion; an almost unthinkable outcome in the twenty-first century.

*

From Armadale on Skye it is a straight run north towards Broadford where the A851 joins the A87 and a sharp right turn north-east takes you to Breakish, Kyleakin and the Skye Bridge. It seems a shame to spend such a short time on the island, so if you are looking for a quick introduction to inner Skye, there is a worthwhile taster on the road north. About 2 miles from the ferry at Armadale, a left turn at Kilbeg takes you on a single-track detour through Tarskavaig, Tokavaig and Ord, eventually re-emerging some 3 miles further north on the same Armadale to Broadford road. At the northernmost point of the road, the River Ord spills into the sea at a gloriously isolated pebble and sand beach. I am particularly envious of the Dualchas-designed house hiding at the edge of the sea behind the rocks which overlooks this scene – a perfect *location, location, location.* I have in mind that all I need I in life is a fly rod, a dog, a Land Rover Defender and this house. I am probably mistaken (and what of the golf you might ask?).

At Kyleakin and Kyle of Lochalsh, the Bridge dominates a landscape that was once only mountains, sea and sky. As you reach its eastern end you briefly take up residence on the island of Eilean Bàn which, with its decommissioned lighthouse, provides a convenient stepping stone for the Skye Bridge as it makes the final leap towards the mainland. An elegant construction it may be, but I do wish it wasn't there. I don't suppose the islanders agree.

Notes

1. The words are from *Day After Tomorrow* written by Tom Waits and Kathleen Brennan in 2004 – the track appears on Tom Waits' album *Real Gone*.

2. A quote from Carl Watkins' *The Undiscovered Country – Journeys Among the Dead*. The book title is taken from Hamlet's soliloquy – *The undiscovered country, from whose bourn no traveller returns.*

Lochcarron

That's me at the weddings, that's me at the graves. Dressed like the people who once looked so grown-up and brave. Judy Collins[1]

Chapter

8

As you travel across the second span of the Skye Bridge to the mainland there is a hill facing you just above Kyle of Lochalsh. On and around this hill weaves the town's golf course; avid students of maps who swing clubs will have spotted the tantalising blue flag marking the spot on the Ordnance Survey.

Sadly, the course has fallen silent; after several unsuccessful resurrections it was finally abandoned in the 1960s, but the evidence of former glories can still be found amongst the undergrowth and when I visited there was even a scruffy white flag attached to a bent stick planted on what was once a much-tended green. Not a flag of surrender but a symbol of sheer bloody-minded optimism, hopefully there is already a restoration committee making plans. The course is positioned to the north of the town on the Plock of Kyle with wide-ranging views towards Skye, and the isles of Raasay and Scalpay on its eastern shore. The small, uninhabited island in the foreground is Eilean a' Mhal which, like many of the small islands, is in the care of the National Trust for Scotland.

The postcard dates from 1931 when Skye was a disconnected island and the ferry still ran between the slipways at Kyle of Lochalsh and Kyleakin. Now, HGVs can swoop onto the island carrying ever more building materials for constructing yet more uninhabited holiday homes in inappropriate places.

GOLF COURSE, KYLE OF LOCHALSH.

Much has changed in the intervening years. The postcard clearly shows the but 'n' ben style white clubhouse and the neat fairways among the rocky outcrops, so much more punishing than mere sand. A dry stone wall stands to the right of the first tee where, hidden in the grass, is a long-forgotten distance marker and a ball cleaner that stands defiantly marking the spot where the Sunday morning dew sweepers once gathered to play for oozle, foozle, ferret and flap penny side bets. The clubhouse *is still there but it isn't the same.*[1]

Before continuing north, it is a rewarding diversion to take a club and some old balls up to the Plock and sky some drives down the abandoned first, dreaming championship golf; the hole is where the ball lands, not that you will see it ever again.

Once over the Skye bridge turn left at the crossroads opposite the old ferry slipway and drive towards Lochcarron, signposted Duirnish and Plockton. The road roughly follows the route of the single-track Kyle of Lochalsh to Inverness railway which the Friends of the Kyle proudly claim is *one of the world's most scenic rail journeys.*[2] The road meanders around the peninsula before eventually picking up the A890 to Lochcarron at Achmore.

The railway stations count down the route along the west side of Loch Carron and, although they are all slightly off the beaten track, they are all worth a diversion: Duirnish, Plockton, Duncraig, Stromeferry and Strathcarron. Plockton Station is grandly maintained with integral self-catering accommodation but it is Plockton itself that is the star attraction with its archetypal Highland main street; rows of symmetrical cottages, two windows up, two windows down and the central front door opening onto the street with, incongruously, palm trees, courtesy of the gulf stream. The street then loops round in the shape of a shepherd's crook to other houses which appear to float on the loch. The scene is overlooked by a red phone box which could have been used for *Local Hero* but wasn't, Hamish Macbeth[3] taking up residence instead; another, more enticing, alternative to dour Pennan. On the right sort of day, the scene is repeated, inverted in the glassy surface of the loch. Perhaps the biggest surprise is that up the hill from the station and behind the high school, there is an airstrip which operates an honesty box for landing fees; trustworthy types these pilots and golfers. Plockton seems to have everything a civilised village needs; everything except a golf course.

The next station along the line is Duncraig which is a request stop originally built to serve Duncraig Castle, another place with an odd history. The castle was built in 1866 by Sir Alexander Matheson who made his fortune from the Chinese opium trade. He was instrumental in extending the Highland Railway through to Kyle of Lochalsh, and it therefore seems reasonable that he should be rewarded with his own private station at the bottom of his garden. During its chequered history it has been a naval hospital, a domestic science college and more recently, home to a reality TV series, *The Dobsons of Duncraig*, a fly-on-the-wall exposé of an extended family struggling to renovate this crumbling pile – *Grand Designs* it was not. However, the quirkiest connection is with Harmony Korine's distinctly odd-ball film, *Mister Lonely,* which was mostly filmed at the castle –

a commune of impersonators go mad in the Highlands. A Michael Jackson look-alike meets Marilyn Monroe, who invites him to her commune in Scotland where she lives with Charlie Chaplin and her daughter, Shirley Temple. I have a perverse fascination for this film, the highlight being the finale when a row of painted eggs sing Iris Dement's *My Life*; or maybe it is Samantha Morton playing Marilyn Monroe as she appeared in *The Seven Year Itch* – yes, I think it is probably the latter. And then, as though a warning from *Pilgrim's Progress*, there is the disturbing sight of Anita Pallenburg (be still my beating sixteen-year-old heart) impersonating the Queen; my, how we change.

The next station is at Stromeferry, once the terminus of the Dingwall and Skye Railway line which opened in 1870. Piers adjacent to the station provided connections with the islands by steamer and a direct route south to Billingsgate Market for the local fishermen. The remains of a substantial railway hotel and the abandoned sidings provide evidence of its bustling past. When the railway was extended to Kyle of Lochalsh, Stromeferry lost its significance, and when the road north from Strathcarron opened in 1970, the ferries came to an end too – *Stromeferry – No Ferry* as the road sign succinctly informs. At least that was the plan, however rockfalls have closed the A890 more than once and the slipways have been pressed back into service. Such are the concerns about further rock falls, there is even the suggestion of a bridge between Stromeferry and North Strome; a potential final indignity for the place, to be overshadowed by another road in the sky. Assuming there are no rock falls, a journey along the A890 keeps close company with the railway line for the final stretch into Strathcarron where the road crosses the line before connecting with the A896; turn left, signposted Lochcarron, Shieldaig and Torridon.

Within 1.5 miles you are suddenly driving through the middle of a golf course. Is there anywhere else on mainland Britain where a golf course traverses an A-road? I have been careful with my choice of words; as I have observed earlier in this book, the 9th at Machrie on the Isle of Arran crosses the A841 twice. And yet, the majority of drivers, riders and walkers press on, oblivious to the potential dangers. This state of mind is based on the false assumption that all golfers are competent and in control of events. If your only exposure is the occasional glimpse of a professional on television then this may be understandable but, it is a distortion. The public should be warned; for the majority of amateur golfers with double-figure handicaps, any connection between intention and result is entirely arbitrary. This gloriously unsettling view up the first at Lochcarron brings this consideration into sharp relief.

Is there a more worrying opener anywhere in the land? How do the locals cope after too many whisky chasers on the previous night? To the left is the unprotected A896 which heads north to Gairloch via Shieldaig, Torridon and Kinlochewe; admittedly single track for large sections and hardly the M6, it is nevertheless alarmingly close at approximately 18 yards to the left of the tee and a few feet from the edge of the fairway. A few paces to the right is the soft, marshy edge of the loch. At its widest point beyond the church, the fairway is just 22 yards from out-of-bounds to water hazard. A par 3, *Jimmy's Seat*, is 210 yards from tee to green, but 126 yards out a burn cuts across the fairway so you need to drive a minimum of 150 straight yards just to be sure of clearing the water. And there is more: the burn arrives under the road parallel with the green and meanders along its bush-lined left edge before looping round into the loch. Finally, the green is elevated, so coming up short is not an option for a shot in regulation. Going for the green is out of the question; my limited armoury simply doesn't include the required golf shot.

I stood on the tee utterly perplexed. This felt more like target practice, archery at a distance far greater than the gents' competition maximum of nearly 95 yards. Short of the green, seemingly beyond the burn to the right, there is an inviting, light patch of turf, so I lined up in that direction, determined to play the sensible shot. I came up too short on the edge of the pebbled burn, punched the ball onto dry land, chipped again to the green and two-putted for five. A hacker's double bogey, ending the hole with the same ball I had started with felt like a minor triumph. I have played this hole twice with exactly the same results; I keep doing the same thing and expecting different results – madness. I find it utterly baffling that this hole is assigned stroke index 9 whereas the stroke index 1 hole seems child's play by comparison; I guess it is bad form to open with the lowest index hole, but the numerical sleight of hand does not make it any easier.

Don't be put off by the description of the first, it is a wonderful setting for golf and on both summer evenings I played, unusually free of the dreaded midge. The first three holes hug the shoreline, the second par 4 taking you on a narrowing approach to the course's most distant green, while the third brings you back to a two-tiered green set in a hollow right next to the road. The fourth, stroke index 1 par 3, is ominously named *The Doctor* – did Valentino Rossi once pass this way?[4] It plays across the third green and, more significantly, across the A-road; beware high-sided vehicles. The fifth, the curious *Flying Ant*, takes you north again towards a small conifer plantation before the remaining holes take you on a circumnavigation of the old church.

The sixth, a par 3, is another slightly unsettling hole; it crosses the stream that wends its way down to the first, there is heavy gorse along its banks, a ditch that runs at right angles to the stream, and tucked away in a corner between the road and the graveyard is a sloping green. No matter how many Prozac you pop, this is an unnerving experience. As you play out this hole and thrust your putter angrily into your bag having missed that simple three footer, take time to peer through the fence into the graveyard and put things in perspective. The second headstone from the left, nearest the road and the green, contains this touching inscription: *In Loving Memory of Annie Mackenzie, Died 4th November 1961, aged 66 years beloved wife of Donald Macrae, Alltachuirn. Died 13th December 1972, aged 90 years. And their only son, Finlay killed in action over Berlin 31st January 1944, aged 19 years – Interred in War Cemetery West Berlin.* Such sad loss, so far from home.

The course plays out with a short par 3 almost parallel to the head-stones, a par 4 along the back of the church and a par 3 which takes you back down towards the car park and the neatly angular wooden clubhouse which sits next to the loch on the other side of the road. You will find it hard to resist going round again unless the first is just too nerve-wracking for a second attempt.

This seems an odd setting for a course established in 1908 and even today it has its repercussions, the course closing when a funeral is being conducted in the graveyard, not the occasion for a wild slice into the head-bent, bible-black mourners. Similarly, competitions are played on Saturdays to avoid expletives echoing across green and shore to enhance the Sunday sermon; this may not be true. Playing golf on Sunday in parts of Scotland is still considered a sinful pastime, but this doctrine is fundamentally flawed, assuming that golf is somehow a pleasurable activity rather than a parallel and complementary religion. We suffer for our sins at pulpit and pin.

At just 1,782 yards (nine holes) and only three par 4s it is undeniably short, but it remains challenging and unusual – just keep an eye out for the traffic and any death notices.

*

We all await the final judgement, but it is the earthly ones that have the more immediate impact. Inquisitive Peg was so practised at judgement that I wonder if there was Spanish blood in the family.

My paternal grandfather, Alfred, was a builder. Brought up in a pub, he had seen the results of the 'evil drink' and was avidly teetotal as was his wife Bessie. My Dad was their only son who arrived late in life: a grammar school boy who was academically successful and fiercely good at games, he went onto London University. He married a shop girl from his home town whose Dad was a well-known local character not averse to the odd pint or three. Was this what Alfred and Bessie wanted for their only son? Significantly, we never once stayed at their contemporary, tidy home, a house in stark contrast to my maternal grandparents'.

It seems almost inconceivable that they did not have an opinion about Fred, May and their shop girl daughter Peg. Was this young girl perceived as not quite good enough for 'our Ken'? Perhaps she aspired to some historical revisionism, to climb the social ladder such that she could, in her turn, sit in judgement on others: the endless cycle whereby the oppressed become oppressors.

My maternal grandparents' house *is still there but it isn't the same.*[5] The small sloping front garden sat above the road held back by a tall flint wall. Opposite, high trees hid the ex-servicemen's home which in the 1950s would still have housed the traumatised of the First World War. The traffic passed by below as if in a cutting as we, the railway children, waved from on high. This was a busy road which led down a steep hill to the town centre, where more than once a lorry with failing brakes would park itself in the bar of a local pub. The road was also the main route south from the army camp a few miles up the road. These heavy vehicles announced their arrival in advance, the whining tinny sound of their tyres on the tarmac louder than the engines that propelled them.

The house was a narrow two up, two down semi-detached the inside proportions of which made it feel more like a mid-terrace. The front door gave onto a narrow hallway with the parlour off to the right; this, the best room, and the front door, were reserved for important visitors and were thus never used. The parlour had two easy chairs, a fireplace, a glass cabinet filled with Goss souvenir pottery and an out-of-tune upright piano which no one except me played, my efforts only confirming the continuing lack of a musical gene in the family. The Goss china was fascinating: souvenirs of Blackpool, Scarborough and Bournemouth sitting alongside a First World War tank, a 'souvenir' from Ypres.

At the end of the short hallway was the living room, a warm nest with a continuously burning coal fire, even in the height of summer. A large, square, red chenille-covered table sat beneath two hunting prints; a dark sideboard was a mess of papers from which emerged a telephone with separate ear and mouthpiece and a delicate glass peacock under a glass dome; a one-day long case clock, forever linked in my mind with Bill Hayley's *Rock Around the Clock*, stood in a corner next to three walking sticks which I would use to adopt a theatrical limp. Two well-worn brown leather armchairs sat astride the fireplace, which was home to a blackened kettle that provided a constant supply of 'free' hot water. Beyond the living room was the dark kitchen lit by a dim bare light bulb. There was an enamel bath covered with a wooden top on which sat random groceries; an unused range; a well-used gas cooker; a Belfast sink with stained wooden drainer and another bare light above a cracked mirror which my grandfather used for shaving with his cut-throat razor. Out the backdoor was a lean-to greenhouse and the outdoor 'privy'. An overhead, over-engineered cast iron cistern was emptied by means of a chain I could just reach by standing on the seat. The warm wooden seat was disconcerting to a young boy raised on cold black Bakelite; no purpose-made paper either, torn squares from the *Andover Advertiser* or *News of the World* providing a rough hard-edged alternative.

Between the front and back rooms, steep narrow stairs climbed across the house to the two almost identical bedrooms; both had brass beds with mattresses that displayed the imprints of their occupants as though they had fallen to sleep from a great height, as though sad Evelyn McHale[6] slept here. Both had sash windows, net curtains hung from wooden poles, long after they had gone out of fashion and long before they returned. In the corner of each was a cupboard full of cardboard boxes – May's hat collection. As May aged she shrank, her knees tired of carrying her upper body those long years so that she became bow-legged, one bending more than the other, resulting in a distinct waddle. It would have been a slow uncomfortable climb to bed up the steep, steep stairs each night before settling into Evelyn's mattress.

In the back garden, a large green water butt collected rainwater from the lean-to greenhouse. A central concrete path stretched the full length of the garden to the chicken coop and Grandad's shed full of dusty mysterious things: unlikely looking tools, tin helmets, gas masks and a rusting gun. It was while tending this garden that Fred collapsed and died from heart failure one cold morning in January 1966. Mum immediately blamed May for *working him too hard* but it now seems a very desirable exit. No prolonged visits to the health professionals, no extended regime of pills and potions each one working against the other, no long, slow, miserable dying of the light in a dusty care home, each occupant shunning the other, too frightened to recognise their own fate in the mirror of someone else's decline. May's judgement day came two years later but, of head-bent, bible-black mourners, there were none.

Notes

1.   The words and music for *Secret Gardens* are by Judy Collins – the track first appeared on the 1973 album *True Stories and Other Dreams*.

2.   I would argue that Fort William to Mallaig is *the* most scenic in the world.

3.   Hamish Macbeth was a comedy-drama series made by BBC Scotland loosely based on the mystery novels by M. C. Beaton (Marion Chesney).

4.   Seven times motorcycle world champion, Valentino Rossi, is nicknamed *The Doctor* because of his calculated and clinical racing style.

5.   From the Judy Collins track – *Secret Gardens*.

6.   On 1st May 1947, 23-year-old Evelyn McHale leapt to her death from the Empire State Building's observation deck and landed on the roof of a car eighty-six floors below. Robert Wiles' iconic photograph of the incident shows an intact Evelyn lying face up as though asleep amid the folds of the enveloping metal, her brief resting place.

To Gairloch

8

*Everything passes, everything
changes. Just do what you think
you should do.* Bob Dylan[1]

T he A896 continues from the golf course along the northern edge
of the Loch, through the village of Lochcarron before heading
north and west through Glen Mor towards Sanachan and Ard-
arroch. As the road turns north on the shores of the sea loch, across
the water, prefabricated industrial units mark the site of what was once
the Kishorn Yard, built and operated by Howard Doris between 1978
and 1985 for the fabrication of oil rigs. It was on these quiet, isolated
shores that the largest movable object ever created by man was born,
the 600,000 ton Ninian Central Platform. How does something that
heavy float? Where would we be without that all too clever Greek,
Archimedes? Given the eventual destination of its major project,
100 miles north-west of the Shetlands, it does beg the question, why
here? At the height of production over 3,000 people were employed
on the site and yet surprisingly little evidence remains of this massive
endeavour, certainly the yard has had much less impact on the landscape than its output. For instance, the site was later used to construct
the footings for the Skye Bridge.

The direct route to Gairloch is north along the A896 via Shieldaig,
just 10 miles north, but the direct passage would miss one of the most
exciting roads in the UK. For just a mile or so beyond Sanachan there
is the left turning for Bealach na Bà, the Pass of the Cattle, the road to
Applecross. The signs at the junction give some clues as to what lies
ahead:

THIS ROAD RISES TO A HEIGHT OF 2053 FT. WITH GRA-
DIENTS OF 1 IN 5 AND HAIRPIN BENDS. NOT ADVISED

FOR LEARNER DRIVERS VERY LARGE VEHICLES OR
CARAVANS AFTER FIRST MILE…it might be qualified
with NOR THOSE OF A NERVOUS DISPOSITION.

The additional signage on the other side of the road falls into the realms
of the self-evident, the 'bleedin' obvious': ROAD NORMALLY
IMPASSABLE IN WINTRY CONDITIONS. This is a 38-mile detour
but worth every precipitous inch.

My first encounter with this road was in the spring of 1973 when there
was still snow at its summit. At the wheel of an 18 cwt Bedford CF
the ascent was somewhat slower than in an Alfa GT nearly forty years
later, but no less exciting. In the intervening years some of the adventure has been diluted by extension of the Armco barriers further and
further down from the summit. It is odd what you remember. Back
in the 1960s when motorway central reservations were unprotected,
there was a series of catastrophic accidents caused by heavy vehicles
crossing into the carriageways of the oncoming traffic. There was
much public debate and within a short space of time metal barriers
were put in place along the centre of all Britain's motorways; nowa-
days we would feel very exposed without them. As part of the debate
leading up to this construction programme, I remember Harry Wheat-
croft, the flamboyant be-whiskered rose grower, offering his services
to plant rosebushes all the way down the centre of the M1. I suppose
it sticks in the mind, not only because of its blatant self-interest, but
also because it would have been wholly ineffective against the might
of a 60-mph ten-ton lorry. Nevertheless, there is no denying that it
would have been much more attractive. Roses along the Pass of the
Cattle would be equally ineffective and wholly out of place in this
wild, wild place but the magnificent gorse bush would satisfy all cri-
teria, aesthetic and practical. As someone who has too often got up
close and personal with such vegetation on a golf course I can vouch
for its sturdiness.

Ironically, for all their grandeur, the warning signs fail to convey the real perils of this road. It is not the height of its summit, it is not the gradient and it is not really the hairpin bends. It is the narrowness of the road, it is the blind corners, it is the limited passing places and in the summer months, the tourists descending in the opposite direction admiring everything but the road ahead.

The road ascends the valley created by Sgurr a'Chaorachain on the northern side and Creag a' Chumhaing on the south. Like the old road at *Rest and Be Thankful*, the final steep ascent is delayed to the last in a series of steep hairpin bends, their saving grace being that anything approaching can be seen descending from the floors above. Just beyond the last hairpin there is space to park and take in the view down Coire na Ba, but be sure to apply the handbrake. The slightly less demanding descent into Applecross has equally impressive and distracting views across to Skye and the Inner Hebrides. Thanks to *Monty Halls' Great Escape*, the 2007 BBC2 TV series, everyone has now heard of Applecross – I am thinking of printing a t-shirt – *I was here before Monty*, long before, in 1973 and many times since. During the writing of this book I have several times concluded that it is near impossible to convey the majesty of landscape in words, there is simply no substitute for being there; I can only recommend that you go see for yourself. My passion for this isolated corner of the world can be best explained by the following short facts. Firstly, it feels like an achievement just getting there, combined with a strong sense of arrival as you coast down into the village. Secondly, the sun always shines on Applecross, no matter what is happening elsewhere – it was shining when I first went there in 1973 and whenever I return, is shining still. Thirdly, it always feels wonderfully removed from the world and I immediately start drawing up plans to relocate. Finally, the landscape and the light are beyond words – see above.

There was a time when Applecross was *the* destination, and apart from a few small hamlets that dot the coastline to the south and the Burial Ground to the north, the end of the road. As one local explains:

Sea transport was far more important. I just caught the end of that era. Ferries to the Outer Isles stopped off and there was the regular Toscaig/Kyle link. My Dad was on that one up till the mid-70s. Fishing was far more important and their boats were used to take in supplies as well. There was a far stronger relationship with the sea than there is now. I suspect that may change back again.

In the late 1970s the through road to the north was completed and the magic of complete isolation was lost. The construction vehicles were visible on the horizon even in 1973, but until I started researching this book, I had never found the time or inclination to go beyond Apple-cross House. When I did it was something of a disappointment; single track with passing places it may be, but for long stretches it is modern and unnaturally straight, cutting through rather than riding over the contours. And then there is Sand Bay where Monty Halls Escaped Greatly; a lovely spot but what the cameras carefully avoided was the British Underwater Test and Evaluation Centre, bang next door, a modern version of the abandoned torpedo station at Arrochar. The Inner Sound, which divides the Applecross peninsula and the Isle of Raasay, was designated a testing range in the 1970s. As well as a torpedo range, the centre also tests the sound characteristics of subma-rines based at Faslane by means of hydrophones placed on the seabed. In war or peace, the lonely places of the northwest seem to attract the activities of the secret and the sinister.

Everything passes, everything changes. The year before I arrived in Applecross I was leading a wholly different life with someone else too carelessly left behind; in July 1972 I hitched through France following the Grand Prix circus down to Clermont Ferrand. In an act of sublime optimism we did the entire trip on £11, relying almost entirely on the good will of the French nation. Armed with advice from a Putney travel agent that *France is a good place to hitch hike*, we based our entire plans on this dubious information. By and large it was only 2CV drivers who responded to our outstretched thumbs; it wasn't that others just drove by, it was the Gallic gestures and insults they felt obliged to shout from their car windows – my schoolboy French was ropey at best, but I am certain it wasn't *Bon Voyage*. They seem a nation of extremes, one half adopting an almost fascist reaction to two young kids trying to get a free ride while others demonstrated extreme kindness to complete strangers. When we arrived late into Clermont Ferrand on the eve of a Grand Prix our last 2CV driver persistently searched the town for a spare room and when this proved unsurprisingly fruitless, he let us bed down in a friend's garret at the top of an ageing office building, something akin to an opium den. The description from my diary of the time is a little more colourful – *six foot square, smelling of hash, swaying in the wind and done up like a voodoo temple, this was home for the night. By the time we hit the sack it could have been Buck house for all it mattered ... it was dry (as long as it didn't rain) and warm (almost too warm) and once asleep this junkie's pad was paradise.* Then, my long-suffering girlfriend needed 'the washroom' that wasn't there – posterity doesn't record what happened next.

The next day Chris Amon drove the race of his life in his Matra Simca MS120, leading the field by 10 seconds before a puncture forced him in for a tyre change. Losing almost a minute in the pits, he rejoined the race in ninth and then drove like a man possessed to finish third. Once again, he confirmed his position as the greatest racing driver to never win a Grand Prix, but he was certainly on fire that day. Talking to fellow Kiwi and sports writer, Norman Harris, some years later he described such occasions like this: *'It's very like 'form' in cricket or golf. But you wouldn't be aware of form when you're driving along a public road, it's when you're driving at the limits – cornering, correcting it as it's sliding rather than just catching it at the end, this is the thing.'*[2] To me, as an avid supporter of Amon, Clermont Ferrand seemed like a turning point; it just felt from there on he was fated never to win a Grand Prix and maybe he felt the same, certainly the fire burned a lot less brightly at Brands Hatch just two weeks later. Nevertheless, he was successful in other branches of the sport, not least winning Le Mans with Bruce McLaren while anyone surviving that era of motor racing can hardly be described as unlucky. When you look at how the cars were prepared for these events you can only wonder at the sanity of all those involved; this oily rag scene looks medieval compared with the operating theatre conditions that prevail in modern Formula 1. The MS120 is not on jacks, it is supported by a couple of spare springs.

The return trip from Clermont Ferrand was no less eventful. On the way out of the circuit we managed to bum a lift north in the Formula 3 transporter belonging to Brian McGuire (1945-1977), sitting high in the cabin playing racing drivers, dreaming all this was ours.

Travelling sedately along a tree-lined highway in the inevitable 2CV we were bumped off the road by a crazy Alfa driver, and in the Paris suburbs we were bundled into the back of a Gendarmes' van for interrogation.

And then a few months later there I am in Applecross pursuing a different life altogether.

*

I prefer the road south from Applecross, which, like Bealach na Bà of old, goes nowhere other than to more hidden places whereas the arrow-straight new road north offers only the views across Inner Sound to Rona as compensation. Eventually the road north begins to twist and turn as it picks up the original coastal tracks to Fearnmore, Kenmore and Ardheslaig, finally reconnecting with the A896 as it heads north through Shieldaig to Torridon. From here the route heads east through Glen Torridon, which in my experience is always a dank and foreboding place, the exact opposite of Applecross; the sun never shines here.

At Kinlochewe it is a left turn north onto the A832, travelling almost the entire length of the glorious Loch Maree before veering west to the coast and Gairloch.

Notes

1. From the final verse of Bob Dylan's *To Ramona* – a folk waltz from his fourth studio album, *Another Side of Bob Dylan*, released in 1964.

2. This quote is from *Fly Away People* by Norman Harris. Norman is an accomplished author and sports journalist who has written for the *Sunday Times*, *The Times* and the *Observer*. He is a long-serving member of the Allendale Golf Club committee.

Chapter 9

Gairloch

*The drone of flying engines
Is a song so wild and blue.*
Joni Mitchell – *Amelia*[1]

O n the approach to Gairloch short stretches of the A832 revert
to single track as a reminder of the way things once were.
However, beyond the turning for Badachro it is full-width
carriageway, downhill, into the village where you are reintroduced to
the sea at Flowerdale Bay and the road to the harbour. Just back from
the road on the right is the original single-track bridge which runs up
to The Old Inn, another reminder of a not-too-distant past. The road
climbs out of Flowerdale Bay, and almost immediately you crest the
rise, Gairloch golf course opens out on the left; this is *Golf in the Wild*
in the heart of the community. The beach and golf club car park are

just 320 yards along on the left which, coincidentally, is the competition length of the first – beware the hooked drive.

Gairloch is pure seaside golf – yes, it is a links course, but it is more than that, it is within sight and sound of a well-used beach. The soundtrack to golf at Gairloch is excitable, shrieking children, the gentle lapping of waves and the barking of frisky dogs taking too much salty air. It is the holidays of my childhood when walks near the beach skirted the local links and very serious ladies and gentlemen in chequered trousers could be seen staring intently at bushes and the long grass as though searching for their lost youth.

There was no playing on the links for us, but there was always the putting green on which to hone my skills, skills I have clearly mislaid since those long-lost summer days. For many years holidays meant Sandbanks on the south coast, west of Bournemouth: familiar territory for my parents raised not so many miles away in Hampshire. In those days Sandbanks was certainly desirable but not the place it has now become – reputedly the fourth most expensive place to live on the planet.

My parents rented the basement, really a cellar, from Sam Margolin, the man behind Dansette, manufacturers of the bright red mono 'portable' record players; nearly every home had one. Sam drove a Bentley, which he parked next to our less-than-ostentatious Ford Consul, and he loved Ray Charles; to be precise he loved one record of Ray Charles – *I Can't Stop Loving You* – which he played loud and long for happy hours, unmuffled despite the intervening floor. I cannot hear the recording without being transported back across the years to that sandy place. Sand was everywhere, blown off the beach, across the road into the shops, in the car parks, in the bed, in the sandwiches, in my shoes and between my toes, but most of the free-ranging dunes have disappeared, replaced by car parks and unaffordable real estate.

Billy Cotton, of *'Wakey Wakey'* fame, who lived on the Poole Harbour side and the recluse Mary Bonham-Christie, who, holed up on her forbidden Brownsea Island floating in Poole Harbour, would not have approved.

It was the family holiday for five successive years when we would travel down in a series of Fords for a month, Dad going back to work one week out of four. This was the highlight of the year, better even than Christmas. The excitement built up for weeks as the end of term approached. At the end of the long journey south down pre-motorway England, approaching the coast you feel its presence long before you see and smell it; you sense it from the bright, sharp light reflecting from the sea, welling up on the southern horizon. Perhaps this is why I was so taken by the northwest; it is not just the landscape but the light that spreads upwards in all directions, from river, sea and lochs, taking me back to summers when the sun always shone.

*

Gairloch course has been open since 1892 and is another overlooked by a church, but unlike Lochcarron it loiters in the wings, shy of centre stage. Nevertheless, it is on the horizon from many tees and provides a perfect backdrop between sea and mountain. The land for the course was gifted by Sir Kenneth S. MacKenzie of Gairloch, 7th Baronet (1861–1929), once described *'as good a Highlander as ever stood in Tartan'*. This kind act was entirely consistent with his reputation as a generous and benevolent landlord. It would be pleasing to imagine the good Sir Kenneth marching to the golf course from the family home at Flowerdale, kilt blowing, sporran swinging, accompanied by mashies, niblicks, jigger and spoons cast idly over one shoulder.

The course is located on what is probably the flattest acreage of links land to be found in the district. It is also quite compact, giving rise to an imaginative layout which not only squeezes in the mandatory nine holes but also includes a challenging par 5. By necessity, fairways cross while tees and greens can be in the line of fire; it is a course where a straight hitter will not only be rewarded on the scorecard but will also avoid abuse from fellow golfers. It is best to have your wits about you when the course is busy.

The 312-yard (yellows) par 4 first, *The Leabaidh*, is the fairway first seen from the road and it looks no less intimidating from the tee than from the passenger seat; Leabaidh must be Gaelic for Laudanum. Therefore, those of a nervous disposition will tend to head right; but down there, out of sight, is a pond or possibly grumpy golfers. The approach is on rising ground to the far corner of the course with bunkers to the left and rear of the green, opposite the conveniently sited Royal Bank of Scotland – it is a pleasing, if slightly worrying, opener. In the first of several such instances, the par 3 second, *Oakwood*, crosses the end of the first fairway at right angles; stray too far left and you are playing into the approach to the fifth; go right and you are in a clump of trees or worse, the pond; go too long and you are on the third tee box. There really is no substitute for a straight shot to the green set atop a mound, like landing a ball on an upturned bowl; it is fun, if testing.

The third 152-yard par 3, *Kirkhill*, heads back towards the church and clubhouse across a ravine to another elevated green. Going right is reasonably trouble-free but left is directly into the path of the par 3 fourth. Again, a straight shot to the seemingly distant green is the preferred solution. My natural tendency to go right seems almost obligatory particularly if there is a group standing on the fourth tee box; an easier and potentially less embarrassing approach than heading left. A shot straight at the green would make the most sense, but that requires a degree of guaranteed competence.

In my experience, a stroke index 2 par 3 is a fairly rare beast, but the 209-yard, *Blind Piper*, is fully deserving of its rating. The tee shot is over a copse of conifers which grow more imposing every time I visit, no doubt inspired by a well-meaning committee decision several decades earlier; it is later generations who suffer while the honourable members languish in that great clubhouse in the sky. To the left is the previous par 3 whilst to the right is the approach to the eighth. By now you should appreciate that this course demands a straight-hit ball from the tee if litigation is to be avoided. Over the hill the ball should collect from the right, but with my limited skill set, hitting this green in regulation is such a rare event that, once achieved, I would walk away never to return, quite certain that the trick could never be repeated. The fifth 312-yard par 4, *Caberfeidh,* is a lovely hole to play and is the second of only two par fours on the front nine. Teeing off from the edge of the eighth fairway (beware balls flying in from the right), the fifth weaves a path between the fourth and sixth before approaching a green carved into the hillside and protected on three sides, an approach that almost demands a lay-up to the left of the green before tackling a challenging up and down.

There is nothing so fine as an elevated tee box, so the beautifully constructed sixth, *Westward Ho!*, with its tee box set high up in the trees, is a delight and my favourite on the course. To the left is uncompromising rough, to the right are trees and to the front are distracting far-reaching views of the Isles – a fantastic par 3. I can only guess that the 1934 photograph shows the view from above the sixth when the primary means of controlling the rough was sheep (the light-coloured blobs).

The 91-yard seventh, *An Dun*, is the shortest par 3 on the course and at stroke index 18, supposedly the easiest. Short it may be, but it is completely blind, the green being hidden by a rocky outcrop which is worrying enough, but beyond the green is the eighth/seventeenth tee box; missing the green is one thing, dispatching a fellow golfer to Inverness Raigmore Hospital quite another.

From the far reaches of the course, the 488-yard par 5 eighth takes you along the edge of the bay, back towards the clubhouse. Just beneath the tee are the remains of target butts used by the Home Guard during the Second World War, the golf course being their rifle range for a large part of the conflict; I assume golf was abandoned for the duration. Among the gallant riflemen was Gairloch's answer to Captain Mainwaring, who was renowned for his bicycle that had machine gun mounts on its handle bars. History does not record if this was ever tested nor the potential effect of the recoil upon the mounted cyclist.

To the left of the 8th fairway is a deep rough and out-of-bounds which, at around two hundred yards, cuts sharply into the edge of the playing surface – another of the course's craters. Going right is tempting, but this just lengthens the hole. I don't know what the locals do, but my intention is always to reach the top of the ravine with my second so that I have clear sight of my third shot, hopefully into the heart of the green. Playing over the ravine from a distance involves too much blind faith and wishful thinking. The green set in the dip between the ninth tee and green looks like God intentionally designed it that way, it is such a perfect setting for a golf hole, surrounded by high dunes. And so to the finish of *possibly the best wee golf course in the Highlands* as the club's tag line commends. The 119-yard finishing hole (139 yards on the front 9), *Mo Dhachaidh,* is named after a long-departed captain's mother. It plays over the approach to the 8th and is another par 3 from an elevated tee to an elevated green, which slopes away from the near edge – it is a very satisfying hole to get right at the end of a round on this delightful course. On my first visit I was fooled into taking too big an iron at the eighteenth and promptly put the ball in the car park – fortunately it was late autumn and empty. There are good reasons for checking the validity of your insurance before playing golf anywhere, but particularly at wee Gairloch.

Both pictures of the course were taken in 1934 and show an entirely recognisable layout, the golfers in the second picture seemingly teeing up for the eighth par 5 as it curves around the bay. It is striking how little has changed in the eighty years since this picture was taken, and probably, little changed in the forty-two years between the establishment of the course and this familiar scene being committed to glass plate. Elsewhere, the world was moving on.

*

A 1965 *Andover Advertiser*[2] profile of my maternal grandfather, Fred Twinn, includes the following paragraph: *'He has always retained his interest in flying and recalls as a young boy acting as a time observer for Colonel Cody's flight between Farnborough, Andover and Newbury'.* Cody was born Samuel Franklin Cowdery in 1867 in Iowa, but changed his surname and adopted the appearance of Buffalo Bill in order to enhance his career as an all-American gun-toting, cattle-roping cowboy and showman.

184

At one stage he even toured Britain promoting himself and his wife, Maud Lee, as Captain Cody and Miss Cody: *Buffalo Bill's Son and Daughter*, until the real Bill sued. Maud then joined another circus, was badly injured, returned to America, became addicted to morphine and ended her days in a home for the insane, leaving the Colonel to take up with an entirely new Madame Cody, Lela King. While aspects of his personal history were pure invention, his life as one of the first aviators was entirely genuine. His first aeronautical exploit involved a kite capable of lifting a man into the sky, which he subsequently sold to the British Army as a reconnaissance device. After a brief foray into airships, he became the unlikely designer, builder and flyer of the first aeroplanes in England. The postcard, which belonged to my grandfather, is captioned *Mr Cody at Lark Hill – Aug 1912.*

Larkhill became the first army aerodrome in 1910 and in 1911 home to the first flying unit of the armed forces which, by May 1912, had evolved into No. 3 Squadron, Royal Flying Corps. The postcard coincides with the August 1912 British Military Aeroplane Competition held at Larkhill and won by Colonel Cody in his Cody V biplane. He was to die a year later at the controls of his latest design, the Floatplane, when it broke up at 500 ft.

A distinctive and romantic figure, an Iowan cowboy admired by Edward VII and George V, he was given a magnificent funeral funded by the War Office – the first civilian to be buried at Aldershot Military Cemetery. In front of his grave there is a memorial stone for his son, Samuel Franklin Leslie Cody 2nd Lieutenant, who, like my grandfather, joined the Royal Flying Corps. *The dear beloved youngest son of Samuel Franklin and Lela Marie Cody ... fell in action fighting four enemy machines in May 1917.* I like to think that the flat-capped civilian in the postcard is Samuel, there appears to be some of the Colonel's facial characteristics in his eyes and profile.

The BBC foreign editor, John Simpson, writes on the subject of Cody in his autobiography, *Days from a Different World*, providing an interesting and insightful family perspective to the story. His maternal great-grandmother was Cody's common-law wife Lela – Madame Cody – *'a bareback rider, a circus performer, a balloonist and (on 14th August 1909) the first woman to fly in an English-speaking country; indeed, she was only the second woman to fly in the entire world'*.

Just five years after his death, at the end of the First World War, there were squadrons of aircraft across the globe and my grandfather spent a good part of that conflict maintaining them at the RFC Training School in Egypt. By the end of the Second World War, these flimsy biplanes had evolved into robust, sophisticated aeronautical devices capable of carrying significant payload and travelling distances unimagined in 1918. There is tragic evidence in the hills above Gairloch.

On 13th June 1945 a battle-scarred B-24 Liberator bomber, serial number 42-95095, had departed from Prestwick en route to Meeks Field, Iceland, for refuelling and an onward journey home to the US. The B-24 Liberator was a four-engined heavy bomber designed in the late 1930s by Consolidated Aircraft Corporation, San Diego; it became the mainstay of US heavy bomber operations throughout the Second World War. The deep fuselage was 67 ft long with a wingspan of 110 ft and the plane was capable of carrying an 8,000 lb bomb load. *Sleepy Time Gal* 42-95095 was assigned the build code of B24-H-25-FO which indicates that it was built under contract by the Ford Motor Company at their Willow Run bomber plant, Ypsilanti near Detroit. She rolled off the production line in early March 1944 and was accepted into service by the USAAF a few weeks later – just over a year after her maiden flight she would come to rest on a faraway Scottish mountain loch where large parts of her remain to this day.

Seriously off-course, it is believed the B-24 clipped Slioch above Loch Maree in bad weather and poor visibility. The plane lost height and circled Gairloch with a burning engine before crashing into Lochan Sgeireach; a little more altitude and she may have managed a survivable landing at sea. In the event, all nine crew and six passengers perished in the ice cold waters and heathered rocky outcrops beneath Sithean Mor; their average age, twenty-five. Germany had surrendered unconditionally on 7th May and within a few weeks the Liberator and these poor boys were on their way home to waiting friends and families in New York, Massachusetts, New Jersey, North Carolina, Kansas, Michigan, Wisconsin, Oregon, Iowa, Texas and Indiana. They are waiting still. The picture shows the remains of one of its four engines, while in the distance a propeller stands upright in the loch like a miniature cenotaph.

Notes

1. These lines are from the second verse of Joni Mitchell's *Amelia,* which is, in part, about the aviator Amelia Earhart; the track featured on her 1976 *Hejira* album.

2. The *Andover Advertiser* was the weekly paper for my parents' and grandparents' home town and was affectionately known as the *Andover Rag.* For many years my maternal grandparents would send a copy to my Mum to keep her up to date with local events. It is still in print today.

9 To Ullapool

Dimmi, dimmi se mai fu fatto cosa alcuna – Tell me, tell me if anything ever got done. Leonardo da Vinci

And still we head north. The A832 follows the coast until it reaches the junction with the Melvaig road where it climbs away from the sea skirting Loch Tollaidh and the northern reaches of Loch Maree. Stretches of the northwest mainland are like fingers reaching for the open sea while the road north follows the path of the knuckles, rising and then falling back to the bays and the salt sea smell of the seaweed-filled shoreline. It is the smell of contentment and the never-ending summers of our childhood.

Growing up is a tapestry of smells that are the first to populate the empty shores of our unsullied memories. They do this more intensely than anything else because, of the five senses, the sense of smell is the most developed at birth. No doubt we are imprinted with the smell of amniotic fluid and our mother's milk, although being too young to remember, the direct association is never consciously retained. My wife's skin has the most intensely reassuring smell I have ever encountered; I find it so safe and so intoxicating that I can only imagine it shares the same chemical make-up as my first memories. I have been under its spell since first we met; basic organic chemistry.

As we move through the planets of the years other smells lodge firmly and become associated with our first experiences: fireworks in the chill November air, chalk dust and plasticine from that first September day at school, Three Nuns pipe tobacco, which invaded every pore of my grandfather, Senior Service, which had the same fatal effect on my Dad, and the hot damp smell of steam trains on foggy days.

As we set off for Clermont Ferrand in the July of 1972 one of our first lifts was in a Morris Oxford – my diary from the time records that it was from *'a gentleman who was passionately reminiscing about the 1938 Donington Grand Prix, the Auto Unions and the Mercedes which smelled of boot polish and made your eyes water'*. This olfactory signature came from the exotic fuel concoctions used to propel these fire-breathing pre-war monsters. For me, as with most racing fans of a certain age, the smell that brings it all back home is inevitably Castrol R. The name Castrol is derived from castor oil, one of the key additives to be found in Charles Wakefield's original creation. Indeed, it is the burning of castor oil that gives it and the race circuits of my memory their glorious and distinctive odour.

Castor oil has long been associated with performance machines and was a primary additive for aero-engines during the First World War. The silk scarves worn by pilots were not an affectation, they were used to wipe excess engine oil from their goggles and also to prevent chafing of the neck caused from constantly looking over their shoulders for enemy aircraft *'at one o'clock'*.

Castor oil is also a very effective laxative which had dire consequences for the bowel movements of early fighter pilots. I like to think that the smell of burning castor oil would have been as nostalgically familiar to my aero-engineer grandfather as it became to me. Does the picture, with my grandfather stood third from the left in the foreground, have the unmistakable whiff of burnt castor oil?

*

Poolewe at the southernmost point of Loch Ewe is in the next bay along the coast as the road heads north. Here the existence of Inverewe Gardens is a reminder that this area benefits from the warm air and sea of the Gulf Stream in its long journey across the Atlantic from Mexico. In my brief experience of the water in these parts I can only say that it has cooled significantly by the time it reaches these Scottish shores. Those posted here in the last war, and there were many, did not write home extolling the virtues of its equatorial climate.

For a time, at the beginning of the conflict, Loch Ewe was used as one of the bases for the Home Fleet; the flagship *Nelson* in the company of *Ark Royal*, *Rodney*, *Repulse* and *Hood* were anchored offshore and visited by Churchill during September 1939.

The *Royal Oak* fatally stayed in Scapa Flow where she was sunk by a German U-boat and remains to this day as a designated war grave. Almost inverted in just 100 feet of water, her hull is about 16 feet beneath the surface. The optimistic intention was to hide the fleet from the German Navy by variously anchoring in the Clyde, at Rosyth, Scapa Flow and Loch Ewe, but none proved safe havens, the entrance to the last-named having been mined by a German U-Boat *U-31* as early as October 1939. On 4th December of that same year HMS *Nelson* struck one of these mines blowing a very large hole on the starboard side and taking her out of commission for seven months.

In the following months and years the sea and coastal defences around the Loch were enhanced with more mines and an anti-submarine boom, anti-aircraft guns, barrage balloons and a significant number of support troops to operate the equipment. Servicemen would eventually outnumber the locals by a factor of three to one, which itself must have felt like a foreign invasion. There were, of course, repercussions: hens that disappeared overnight, a shortage of beer glasses in the pubs obliging servicemen to provide their own jam jars and, perhaps most alarming of all, the night someone 'accidentally' fired an anti-aircraft gun from HMS Bermuda.[1] The shell travelled 2 miles, killed a sow and two piglets and ejected a surprised, but unharmed, baby from its pram. It is hard not to imagine the local Corporal Jones being involved in this episode – *don't panic Captain Manwairing!*

By early 1942 Loch Ewe had become established as the gathering anchorage for the Arctic convoys, a total of nineteen comprising four hundred and eighty-one merchant ships and over one hundred naval escort vessels departed these quiet shores for the perils of the North Atlantic. The last sailed on 30th December 1944 marking the end of a three-year endeavour that had cost one hundred merchant ships and over eight hundred lives. After years of campaigning it was finally announced in 2012 that veterans of the Arctic convoys would be awarded their own medal; about bloody time.

Little evidence remains of this area's significant role in the Second World War although in a lay-by on the road north, just before Ault-bea and the turning for Mellon Charles, there is a storyboard which chooses to ignore the obvious legacy: cranes and a jetty that mark the location of the NATO Z-Berth where nuclear submarines emerge from the depths for servicing. If the sight of the occasional nuclear sub in these quiet waters seems sinister, this is nothing in comparison to the activities that took place in the next bay.

The A832 continues its relentless path north over high, empty moorland and then hugs the coast of Gruinard Bay before descending again to the shoreline. Occasional traces of the old single track road provide evidence of a much more spectacular descent before the new road was dynamited out of rock. The road swoops around a lonesome bay cutting between Torr Mor and Carn na Caillich and arriving at the Gruinard House Estate beyond the Gruinard River. From this coast road, between the trees, can be seen Gruinard Island about a mile from the shore. In the 1970s, when I first travelled these roads, blood-red MOD signs warned the inquisitive traveller, for good reason, to KEEP OUT and not to attempt to land on the island.

In late 1941, fearing the Germans were developing biological weapons, scientists from the chemical warfare establishment at Porton Down visited the island and exploded a canister containing concentrated anthrax next to tethered sheep and cows; within a few days they were all dead. The exercise was repeated by dropping a small anthrax bomb from a low flying Wellington with similar devastating results. Not surprisingly, the consequences were not entirely confined to the island as dead sheep floated across the bay and infected the local stock. The island was not cleaned up until 1987 when the MOD hired a contractor to spray the area with a mixture of formaldehyde and sea water enabling the ominous signs to be taken down and the island declared safe three years later. Not many visit. Shortly after the clean-up exercise a spire was erected on the island by the social sculptor George Wyllie (1921–2012) with a plaque declaring *'For air, stone and the equilibrium of understanding. Welcome back Gruinard'*. As a young sailor in the Royal Navy, Wyllie walked among the charred city of ruins, Hiroshima. There are bleak parallels with Gruinard Island. The Japanese city was the first place to suffer an atomic bomb and this small, Scottish island was the first place in the world to be subjected to biological warfare – *Dimmi, dimmi se mai fu fatto cosa alcuna.*

193

Wyllie's spire is a very basic structure with a vertical rod counter balanced by a stone and set in a tripod to allow free movement like the sails of a ship. He considered this spire his favourite artwork from a five-decade long career, declaring in his final interview: *'I like my little spire, my little vertical wand responding to the earth and the air.'* I like to imagine it fluttering still as I write these words, many miles from that lonely, infected isle.

*

The road becomes emptier and lonelier as it sweeps along the south side of Little Loch Broom and winds along the path of the Dundonnell River with its softer landscape. The road eventually joins the A835 at Braemore Junction some 18 miles southwest of Gruinard; sometimes you are obliged to travel many miles south in order to eventually travel north, such is the shape of the northwest coast. From here it is a 12-mile straight stretch along the northern side of Loch Broom to Ullapool.

Notes

1.   This story is from Steve Chadwick's *Loch Ewe during World War II.*

10 Ullapool

Sons of the great or sons unknown
All were children like your own.
Jacques Brel - *Sons of ...* [1]

Ullapool feels like a frontier town, the last outpost before the far north begins. In the 1980s when Russian fishermen roamed the streets, half-repaired Ladas were parked on the decks of visiting trawlers and factory ships moored off the Summer Isles, it felt like the Wild West. But then the fisheries collapsed and the Russians went home. As a local fisherman has written:

When I was a young lad my father, along with thousands of
others, was employed in the herring fishing on the West coast,
this fishery has now gone. The white fishery which employed

hundreds has now also collapsed there. These West coast fisheries were not the victims of unforeseen events or natural disasters, the cycle was the same both times, the fisheries became overdeveloped due to hungry markets and better technology, and stocks went into decline. Lack of supply to the market made it viable for the larger and better financed vessels from elsewhere to fill the gap, causing these fisheries to collapse. The only fishery left on the West coast which employs significant numbers of people is prawns and there are signs that history is about to repeat itself.

Ullapool seems to thrive nonetheless, its wealth presumably built on tourism, both local and those passing through on the ferries to the isles. I have spent many a night in the town under canvas, in the bunkrooms attached to the Ceilidh Place and, more recently, in B&Bs along West Shore Street; it never disappoints. The golf course is on the north side of the town on the left of the A835 immediately after the cemetery. The entrance is not a grand affair with a car park that is flat and over large, a modest clubhouse that could be Allendale's and a flat fairway that runs off in the distance towards a housing estate. It feels almost urban and very un-Highland like, but do not be fooled, magic waits around the corner. The dogleg first par 4 is something of a tester for the uninitiated. There is out-of-bounds and scrub down the left, bushes in front of the housing estate, which look closer than two hundred yards, and to the right, an uninviting plantation which appears to be surrounded by a ditch – although this was empty after a long, dry winter on the occasion I visited. If you can keep straight and long it is a relatively short pitch to the green, but go too far left or right and your eventual destination remains a mystery. The putting surface is elevated and narrow – approach from the intended direction and there is some green to play with, but approaching from either side can make for some repetitive chipping and an ugly start.

A short walk between trees to the second and you emerge on an elevated Highland tee with all the grandeur you could wish for; any hint of the urban has now disappeared. The tee sits high above the Ullapool River to the left with deep Loch Broom to the rear of the par 3 green, some 180 yards from the whites (which are played on the front 9) and 138 yards from the yellows (played on the back 9). From the yellows you can see the fate of your shot as it climbs high into the air and drops to the distant green below – from the whites, its fate is more difficult to estimate. This is *An Teallach*, named after the mountain that overlooks Little Loch Broom and is presumably visible from the tee, but not on the day I played. It is the perfect antidote to the first and a good indication of the joys to come.

The third, *Loch Broom*, a 338-yard par 4, plays along the water's edge with a high gorse bank along the landward side. It was here that I was fortunate to bump into Kenny, the greenkeeper's Dad, who explained the significance of the white and yellow tees on the front and back 9, guided me around the course and generally made this maiden voyage a delight. Local knowledge and good company make all the difference and suddenly my game picked up as the element of guesswork was removed. I even managed to find this tight green in regulation, but of course promptly three-putted.

The fourth is another gloriously elevated par 3 playing into the far corner of the course, again, squeezed between shore and hillside gorse – beware of blissfully unaware walkers dreaming along the shoreline – both are easily within reach of the hooked tee shot. The hole is named after the *Summer Isles* which are visible to the northwest from the tee, the largest of the islands being Tanera Mòr, accessible by ferry from Achiltibuie in the summer months. I have 'previous' with the Summer Isles having first visited Tanera Mòr one bright summer day on the local ferry; a few years later we dragged our three young boys back to a remote cottage in Culnacraig at the very end of the end of the road that runs along the shoreline through Achiltibuie to the foot of Ben Mor Coigach. The cottage had distant connections with Lucy Irvine of *Castaway* fame whose father once owned the local Hydroponicum; it would have been good training for a desert island life, being at the very epicentre of nowhere. Enduring harsh weather and with *'nothing to do'*, two of the boys have been cured of ever wishing to return to Scotland despite their half-Scottish bloodline.

Apart from the similarity with seaside light, I am unsure where I acquired the desire for such out-of-the-way places. There is no history of such desires on my side of the family, indeed, apart from one brief summer holiday in Cullen, my parents had never ventured north of Newcastle.

*

My maternal grandmother, the previously mentioned Mrs Kipper, had three brothers, Albert, Charles and Frederick. Albert and Frederick were never discussed, but whenever Charlie's name came up there was much heaving of bosoms and silent mouthing. I saw him but once; a Chaplinesque figure appeared at my grandparent's back door, there was a brief conversation and he went. He was not invited in.

Charlie collected postcards, the first incarnation of the simple text message. I have about sixty, all dating from before the First World War. Most messages are shorter than a tweet and convey little about the sender or recipient. In a cramped space and a scrawling hand the majority can be summarised as *Thanks for the postcard, hope you are well, I am fine, weather is awful, write again soon.* The cards are addressed to Charlie at two different addresses: *62 Montague Square,* and *31 Phillimore Gardens, South Kensington,* both in London.

And then there is this one from the unknown 'Mabel', which in one small c/o explains a life in service:

To:
Mr Taylor
c/o Sir R Finley (sic)
Newton House,
Nairn Scotland

Dear Charles
I am away for my holidays in Norfolk. This is the waterfall belong-
ing to the lake on the gentleman's estate where I am staying. We
often go fishing. I hope you are having a nice time
Love from Mabel
Stradsett Hall Gardens
Nt Downham Mkt
Norfolk

Charlie, in a real-life version of Downton Abbey, must have worked below stairs for Sir Robert Finlay (11 July 1842 – 9 March 1929), a British lawyer, doctor and politician who became Lord Chancellor of Great Britain. The 62 Montague Square address is Sir Robert's London address and Newton House his summer residence at Nairn, his constituency.

David Thomson (1914–1988) was a writer and BBC radio producer, and, by fortunate coincidence, I have read his autobiography – *Nairn in Darkness and Light*. Given the title of the book, I took it down from the shelf and scanned the first few pages for any possible references to Newton House. Then the penny dropped: David's mother was a Finlay, so when he writes *The Great Panjandrum was my name for our great-uncle Robert, whom I feared and loved*, he is writing of Sir Robert Finlay. When he writes of life below stairs he is writing of a world very familiar to Charlie:

> *Twenty or thirty people waiting for prayers stood by the walls*
> *and windows underneath the huge portraits of relatives and*
> *guests of the past, waiting for Uncle Robert. No one dared*
> *to touch a morsel before prayers. When he was ushered in by*
> *Gulliver, 'that English butler', he stood for a moment near the*
> *door, glancing around the room to make sure, I suppose, that*
> *none of us was missing, said, 'Good morning' in a loud clear*
> *voice, walked over to the lectern and stood before it in silence,*
> *his back to the windows, until all the servants had quietly filed*
> *into the room and assembled near the great sideboard.*

This is a vanished world, Charlie's world, and a world where the journey to Newton House at Nairn was as regular as the seasons. All is not gone however. Newton House still stands, converted to an hotel since 1951 and the grounds still border *The Great Panjandrum's* other fine legacy which he created in 1887 – Nairn Golf Club. It is reassuring to realise that at least one of my ancestors was familiar with Scotland and wild golf, so maybe the love of the two was passed down in the genes from May's side of the family – maybe Mrs Kipper was not such a bad old trout after all. Teasingly, the Newton Hotel was once a favourite haunt of the real Chaplinesque figure, Chaplin himself.

*

At the fifth, Ullapool's course heads south across the *Gully*, a temptingly short uphill par 4 to a green bordered by fearsome gorse, so while a par should be on the cards it is wise not to be too long. It was here that we came across Kenny's son tending the green in his own world, MP3 player plugged into his ears to overcome the sound of the strimmer, golfers, golf balls and his approaching Dad. Dad the golfer who helps out on the course, his son the greenkeeper – it is reassuring to see strong family traditions. Like father, like son.

*

This proud man in his fireman's uniform is my great grandfather, Charles Benjamin Buscall Deaves Twinn, my maternal grandfather's father (1864–1937).

He is dressed in the uniform of the Andover Fire Brigade – Fireman No. 12; helmet, buckle and buttons shining, his hand rests upon his fireman's axe. I am certain this was taken in 1923; there is a group picture of the Fire Brigade in C. J. J. Berry's *Old Andover* – 340 pictures covering 120 years, published in 1976. In the book, Charles is standing in front of a fire engine in identical uniform and pose, looking exactly the same age. *'Andoverians took great pride in their Fire Brigade which was under the direct control of the Borough Council. For 33 years from 1903 to 1936, its highly respected commander was Capt. F.A. (Arthur) Beale, of Beale & Sons, the local builders and*

under him the Brigade had a fierce esprit de corps and excelled in
efficiency and in competitive drills, winning dozens of trophies and
diplomas'.

I imagine Fred and May calling at his father's house just before he
goes for the group photograph, May heavily pregnant with my mother,
born in August 1923. Charles' wife Alathea:

*'Doesn't your Dad look grand Fred, go on take his picture. I can't
believe it, he will be sixty next year and then he is finished with the
Brigade, my, doesn't time fly. There will be a vacancy coming up Fred,
perhaps you could take his place when he retires – the extra money
would come in handy now you've got May and the baby to think of'.*

Sure enough, Fred's 1966 obituary includes the following: '*During
World War II he was a full-time fire officer in the Andover Fire Brigade, having joined in 1925 and served until 1945. He was called to
help at the blitzes at Portsmouth and Southampton'.*

This second picture appears to be just a bunch of 'old boys' gathered round some up-turned boxes drinking tea, maybe laced with

something stronger; my grandfather, Fred, is seated second from the left. Look more closely and at least two are in the uniform of the Andover Fire Brigade (AFB badges) while one blackened individual looks fresh from an inferno. On the far right of the picture, on the ground next to the bucket, is a rolled-up fire hose.

Is this photograph the morning after, have they just returned from war-torn Plymouth or Southampton or has there been a more local tragedy? C. J. J. Berry's book states: *'A solid-tyred Dennis engine was bought in 1927 and converted to pneumatic tyres in December 1933'.* Charles and Fred would have both been familiar with this machine. *'The first big fire it attended after conversion being that at the Heronry, Whitchurch, a country mansion blaze in which two died; the Duc de la Tremoille and Capt. the Hon. J.H.B. Rodney'.* The *Andover Advertiser* report on the fire includes this chilling detail: *The finding of the charred remains of Prince Louis Jean-Marie de la Tremoille, premier Duke of France, was told by Supt. S. Bennett, of Andover. The chauffeur, Jackson, said Capt. the Hon. J. H. B. Rodney was apparently not seriously injured after his leap from the window, and it was a surprise that he died soon after admission to hospital.* It seems certain that Fred would have been in attendance that tragic night. Like father, like son.

*

As we stand on Ullapool's sixth tee, the par 4 *Terraces*, Kenny junior appears on his tractor, still plugged in as his Dad drives a fine ball up the dogleg left that takes you on to a green near the first and the bend in the Ullapool River – it is another relatively short hole which should invite a par. Uncharacteristically, I two-putted for a par in and out – this is how an otherwise unremarkable hole becomes a 'firm favourite'.

Once beyond the first the landscape has all the appearances of a mature course which has hosted golf for many a season, thus belying its relatively recent origins. It was opened in 1998 by Prince Andrew, a highly competent golfer whose four handicap would qualify him to take up the sport full-time and become a member of the Professional Golfers' Association. The Prince is obviously a Royal with too much time on his hands – like father, like son. In a gesture with colonial overtones he donated a trophy to the club to be played between Ullapool and Stornoway on an annual basis with the proviso that it must be played on a Friday 13th over 13 holes. This sporting diplomacy is reminiscent of an inter-island cricketing trophy he once donated in the West Indies which had the effect of bringing peace to once-warring factions; perhaps he should provide a competition trophy for Newcastle and Sunderland – no hope with Manchester and Liverpool – the scousers would pinch the trophy after the first event (says a Mancunian).

Unfortunately there is a downside to the Prince's generosity; while there can be up to three Friday 13ths in any one year, they do not necessarily fall at suitable times of the year and there can be gaps of up to 14 months between occurrences. I imagine that the Committee has some fun scheduling this event.

Intriguingly, the history of Gairloch golf course includes this reference to Ullapool – *'This fledgling club played its first match against another club in late 1899 when Ullapool Golf Club were its guests'*. There is little evidence of the previous course, which was sited near the old Morefield Hotel, now a housing estate just south of the new facility, but look closely and there are tantalising elevations in the nearby park, which suggest the outlines of long-lost bunkers and greens. Sadly, there will have been a good number of years when golf at Ullapool was just a distant memory for the old members, although clubs and courses are not necessarily interdependent – golf clubs without a course are not without precedent. Alsager Golf Club on Linley Road north of Kidsgrove in Staffordshire famously has a splendid clubhouse but no course for its members to play on. The adjoining land was returned to agricultural use in 1953, but as the members owned the building and the land it stood on, they have kept it running as a private members' club ever since.

At 378 yards, the seventh is the longest of the par 4s. A slight dogleg right, a well-struck drive will put hedges on the left and bushes on the right within range and thus demands a straight tee shot. The second is mostly blind to a target post set behind the green, which sits down in the dip. A shortish iron will let the ball roll down the slope into the heart of the green, assuming the ground beneath your feet is dry. The extra carry from the slope puts this longest par 4 in regulation reach of even the average hitter of the ball.

The eighth, a challenging par 5, takes you back towards the clubhouse in a dogleg left. The appropriately and succinctly named *Long* is played from a tee box set back among the bushes – not a place to top your drive. Left is out-of-bounds while a plantation and the seventh fairway are to the right; going long and right is usually safe enough but straight is better – usually, but not always the case. A good fairway wood along level ground and a solid pitch will take you to a flat green and a 'certain' par. The remainder should be easy. At the 300-yard par 4 ninth – shorter from the whites, there is out-of-bounds to the left but plenty of room to play with on the right; again a solid pitch should get you to the *Rowan Over* green in regulation, but there is a sting in the tail. The two-tiered green is very difficult to read and it is not hard to imagine the potential for some evil pin placements. Kenny told the tale of many a ruined card at the eighteenth. At one club champion-ship it so destroyed a possible winning card that the poor victim never played again. It has also been known to reduce a lady playing member to tears and probably grown men, if truth be told. Happily I survived, two-putting on both occasions to retain my sanity and my clubs for the final rounds at Durness.

Notes

1.   *Sons of ... (Fils de)* appears on *Jaques Brel 67,* released in January of that year.

The Last Lap

*The muses are ghosts and some-
times they come uninvited.*
Stephen King – *Bag of Bones*[1]

It is left out of the Ullapool Golf Club car park and full tilt to the very far north – well, full tilt with diversions. From here on the landscape turns to true wilderness and the continuing quest to play *Golf in the Wild* seems an unlikely proposition. The road north progresses in a series of Ansel Adams photographs that imprint themselves on the silver bromide emulsion of the brain. The first exposure is the majestic sweep of Ardmair Point projecting towards Isle Martin and Ben Mor Coigach on the horizon. The road drops to sea level, follows the stony beach and the precarious houses that line the bay before climbing towards Strath Canaird. Just after crossing the River Canaird there is a signpost to Blughassary along a single track road deemed 'Unsuitable for Buses' and much else. This is the route of the *Postie Walk* that takes the intrepid and unsuspecting along a coastal path to Achiltibuie and the Summer Isles. The story is that a local postman would do this walk every day without fail to deliver the mail to these distant communities. I can only say that if I was assigned the job I would be dead within the week. My one experience of this route with my eldest son and in one direction only, from Strath Canaird to Culnacraig, put me in bed for two days. Admittedly it was in a howling gale and I think we lost the intended route quite early on, but nothing could ever persuade me to make a second attempt.

Three miles further on is the first of the almost obligatory detours. You would not wish to travel this far and miss it; take the turning left at Drumrunie, signposted Achiltibuie, 15 miles. The road soon diminishes to single track across an empty landscape, which is only occasionally interrupted with clusters of trees marking lonely homesteads; otherwise there is nothing but gorse, heather, bog, water and mountain. This is an empty place where the wildlife seems particularly shy; having spent a long cold day not catching wild trout in these lochs, I have personal experience that the submerged life is equally recalcitrant.

The road skirts Creag Dhubh and Cul Beag as it joins the eastern reaches of Loch Lurgainn and the next exposure is imprinted on the brain – Stac Pollaidh. This is a relatively small mountain and doesn't rate as a Munro but it grabs your attention immediately because it is shaped like an upturned jelly mould and stands quite alone in the landscape – once seen never forgotten. The road skirts its southern slopes and a convenient car park gives access to a well-trodden path to the summit; there are no hour-long treks across open moorland just to start the ascent. And the climb is worth the effort; from its isolated summit there is the best view possible south to the Summer Isles and to the north Cul Mor, the majestic Suilven, Canisp and Quinag dominating the Assynt landscape – *all children of the same primeval family, standing like silent sentinels of time which have withstood the desolations of incalculable ages* – T. Ratcliffe Barnett – *Autumns in Skye Ross and Sutherland,* 1930.

Loch Lurgainn narrows and then joins Loch Bad a Ghaill, providing a shoreline drive to the junction at Badnagyle where a right turn heads north into the Inverpolly Nature Reserve and, ultimately, Lochinver. This has to be one of the top ten drives in the world, the ever-winding single track ensures there is no rushing through *this* landscape. Within a short distance the ridged peaks of Suilven come into view, the symmetrical dome at its western end providing a constant signature throughout the journey north across the reserve. The dome, Caisteal Liath, keeps slipping into view and in the evening the western setting sun will set its dark red slopes afire, a sight as spectacular as any northern light – exposure number three.

For long stretches this is an inland drive until the road descends to Loch an Eisg-brachaidh where you drive as close to the sea as you can without getting your tyres wet, a low stone wall affording little in the way of reassurance. In April 1973, along this stretch, many summers ago and against local by-laws, we parked up our Bedford van in a passing place for the night, waking in the morning to the brightest sky and sea I can remember; some rules are made to be broken.

An empty 18 cwt van has drawbacks as a mobile home; the lack of insulation means you wake to condensation dripping from the roof while the freezing night rises through the cold steel floor to penetrate the warmest of sleeping bags, but I don't remember caring. We were young, bursting with energy and full of high ideals. We shared a passion for life, wild places and a disobedient but intensely affectionate Irish setter who, in a moment of inspired scientific endeavour, once proved that sheep are very competent swimmers. Out of sight of the Highland shepherd, the dog survived the experiment, as did the sheep.

As the road descends to the bridge over the River Kirkaig, Ross and Cromarty is left behind and Sutherland begins: the beginning of the extreme north. Just over the bridge on the right is the path to Achins, one of the more remote bookshops on mainland UK, and below that the path to Inverkirkaig falls, a manageable 4-mile hike to the edge of Highland wilderness. The road then hugs the river on its journey to the sea before curving around the bay at Inverkirkaig, a relative metropolis complete with its own phone, post box and a scattering of houses. This settlement is followed in short order by Badnaban and Strathan before the final descent into the fishing port of Lochinver. From here the road sweeps westward between Loch Assynt on its south side and Quinag to the north before reaching the junction with the A894 at Skiag Bridge where a left turn is signposted Kylesku, Scourie, Kinlochbervie and, finally, Durness, journey's end.

Before turning for the north there is another worthwhile diversion along the edge of Loch Assynt; if you ignore the turning north and continue for another half mile you will soon see the remains of Ardvreck Castle set on a small island connected by a strand of shingled beach to the shoreline. The castle dates from the fifteenth century and was once home to the Macleod's of Assynt; as with all these islanded gaunt remains, it has a bloody history. At the beginning of the twentieth century, the area was put to a more civilised use. Just before the Great War, the Duke of Sutherland's grandson, the enterprising Eric Chaplin, designed and established a nine-hole golf course on the stretch of land between the castle and the remains of Calda House to the east. It was maintained by the lone greenkeeper, James Mackenzie, with his one-horsepower cutter and rollers, a one-man band who also ensured collection of the golfers' one shilling green fees; in many ways the same business model employed by modern nine-hole courses.

Stand by the ruins[2] and imagine golfers in plus fours, mashies and niblicks in hand; a group is disembarking from the hissing steam ferry which carries guests from the Loch Assynt Lodge across the water's mirrored surface in a bright Highland light to the jetty by the castle. They make the short journey to the first, pay their shilling to the hard-working James and after a short discussion on side bets, tee up and drive towards Calda House around the bay. The first to strike the ball slices into the Loch; the second runs straight down the centre line of the fairway and the third drifts left into the rough that James has let grow too long, a deliberate ploy designed to separate the men from the boys. However, these boys are easy-going and care little about setting a score; they are privileged, they have their lives before them, and everything they do is undertaken with carefree abandon and enthusiasm. One year later they will remember this bright Highland day as, with the same boyish enthusiasm, they board the boat for France and the front line. The Ardvreck Castle course is possibly the finest example of *Golf in the Wild* to be found anywhere on the planet – how I wish it remained.

It is fitting that the final stretch north along the A894 starts with a long ascent thereby feeding a childhood misconception that all roads north should, with the exception of the odd dip, go uphill. It is a misconception that has not entirely left me. When travelling northwards on canals I am always convinced there is a slight incline, an even more absurd scenario.

At Unapool the road descends to Kylesku where once a ferry with a rotating deck transported up to six vehicles at a time over Loch Glendhu. This was still in operation in 1973 when first I passed this way and I distinctly remember that the single track 'A' road on the north side had grass growing down its centre. Now a bridge flies traffic over to Kylestrome in seconds without even a passing nod to the once vital outpost of Kylesku; progress of sorts, I suppose. Drive down into Kylesku today and, pleasingly, the slipway and hotel remain. At Scourie the land temporarily softens and for a short stretch there are even street lamps, surely a misguided use of hydroelectric power; the summer nights are so short they can hardly be needed and the winter nights so long and bleak you wonder why anyone would want to venture out. If they do, Scourie is not exactly the murder capital of the northern hemisphere.

The road runs down to the sea again at Laxford Bridge and then heads north to Rhiconich where the road to Kinlochbervie provides the excuse for yet another diversion. Through Inshegra, Badcall, skirting Kinlochbervie and following the signs for Oldshoremore, the road eventually reaches Blairmore and an unusually large car park for such an out-of-the-way place. Opposite is the start of the hike to Sandwood Bay, about 4 miles out and 4 miles back. This was once a very lonely and desolate place, but the size of the new parking facilities suggests that walkers can now expect company, welcome or otherwise. In April 1973 we were absolutely alone, almost.

The terrain is on the level for most of the route and dry except for the outflows from Loch na Gainimh and Loch a Mhuilinn. To the west the sea is hidden by rising ground and to the east there is seemingly endless moorland stretching into a vast, empty wilderness. As the walk approaches Sandwood Bay the change in landscape is dramatic and a relief. Heavy Atlantic breakers pound a wide-arcing beach that stretches for over 1½ miles from northeast to southwest. The sands rise from the sea to a ridge of dunes and then fall away again to a saltwater lagoon; behind that sits the freshwater Sandwood Loch with its roofless, eyeless cottage. Beneath the quick and shifting sands lie the wrecks and their sailors washed upon these shores before and since Stevenson's guiding light steered ships away from Cape Wrath. Unsurprisingly, this land is haunted with the ghosts of these ill-fated seamen, some Viking, some from an Armada galleon, the ghosts of crofters and those who came for escape and travelled no further. All of these lost souls are presided over by the giant sea stack, Am Buachaille, the Herdsman, standing imperious at the southern end of the sands. I love this corner of the world, but nothing would persuade me to sleep overnight near its shores.

It was long ago but I am sure I remember this much. Across the open moorland to the right of the well-trodden path a rough-bearded, dishevelled man was heading steadfastly north with carrier bags in each hand. A few hundred yards behind two policemen followed at the same pace, not giving chase, just slowly gaining ground. They progressed north as we progressed south so the outcome is unknown. It was 1973 so this was almost certainly James McRory-Smith who lived for thirty-two years at Strathchailleach bothy, 1½ to the north of Sandwood Bay; *an empty corner of an empty land* – Mike Cawthorne, *Wilderness Dreams*. By reputation, the carrier bags probably contained Carlsberg Special Brew, James' weakness. An ex-soldier who served in Germany and married with two children, he never recovered from the loss of his wife who died in tragic circumstances. After leaving the army he eventually turned up at Durness where, for a while, he lived in an abandoned schoolhouse on the east side of the Parph, the area of land to the west of the Kyle of Durness which encompasses the lighthouse and the MOD bombing ranges. From here he migrated to Strathchailleach where he survived for more than thirty years in determined isolation until ill health eventually forced him to live out his remaining years at Kinlochbervie. He is buried at Sheigra cemetery, at the end of the road from Blairmore, within sight of the sea and within walking distance of Strathchailleach; I feel sure he wanders this empty land still.

*

I did not set out to write a ghost story but this book is haunted from beginning to end. Not least there are all those heroes of my teenage years who met tragic ends yet remain alive in memory: Jim Clark,

213

Jochen Rindt, Ronnie Peterson, Jo Siffert, Bruce McLaren, Piers Courage, Pedro Rodriguez, Paul Hawkins, Mike Spence and far too many others. It seems only fair that fate should spare the man who did so much to improve Grand Prix safety, Jackie Stewart. His views were not always welcome, as he was only too aware – '*I would have been a much more popular World Champion if I had always said what people wanted to hear. I might have been dead, but definitely more popular*'. That year, 1973, marked his third and final world championship.

Examine the fate of those who survived into retirement and a chilling number could still not escape death's cold grip: *There was, I knew, a certain scheme of natural balances wherein a gift of fortune rarely arrives without setting the style for a subsequent penalty* – Ernest K. Gann – *Fate is the Hunter.*[3] Mike Hawthorn, only months into his retirement from racing, died in a car accident on the A3 Guildford bypass; Graham Hill retired from racing in early 1975 to concentrate on running his own team – he was killed when his light aircraft crashed near Elstree later that same year; Carlos Pace was in his fifth year of Grand Prix racing when he was killed in a light aircraft accident in early 1977; Didier Pironi retired from Grand Prix racing following an accident in 1982 – he was killed in an offshore powerboat race in 1987; Mike Beutller survived three years of Grand Prix racing for Clarke-Mordaunt-Guthrie but died young in 1988 from complications resulting from AIDS; James Hunt survived on the track but died from a heart attack aged only forty-five.

And then there were those who possessed so much of life's good fortune that to seek more was perhaps too tempting for fate. François Cevert had been Stewart's obedient number two at Tyrrell since 1970 and for 1974 he had the prospect of finally achieving number-one status within the most successful team of the era. He had everything to live for, the championship would be his for the taking. I had followed this king-in-waiting from his early days in a Tecno Formula 2, the first year in the Tyrrell-run March 701 and then the golden years in the Cosworth-powered, Derek Gardner-designed Tyrrells. He was the height of French-cool:

> *François was a young man 'Beloved of the Gods' if ever there was one. The most striking thing was the deep, shimmering blue of his eyes which seemed to shine through even the darkened visor of his blue crash helmet. Almost throughout his racing career he was to enjoy the legendary Napoleonic touchstone of luck* – William Court – *Grand Prix Requiem.*

In 1971, with Stewart's championship already in the bag, Cevert achieved his only Grand Prix victory at the last race of the season, the US GP at Watkins Glen in New York State.

When he travelled there two years later under identical circumstances did he already believe this race was his, that somehow he owned this victory, he was *destined* to win? There is documentary footage of Cevert and Stewart discussing gear changes just prior to the second practice session – significantly, they are in disagreement about which should be used through the rough and blindingly quick Watkins Glen Esses. The stubby 1973 Tyrrell was a twitchy animal which Stewart controlled through this corner by using fourth gear, slower but more driveable – *'you always over-gear a nervous car'*. Cevert was taking the corner flat out in third and, although 0.75 seconds slower than Stewart in the first session, as he told Ken Tyrrell, he went out in the second determined to get on pole. Ken Tyrrell said later, *'it wasn't to be. He just lost it. The car went between the two guard rails and forced them apart.'* Stewart was utterly overwhelmed, *'I was so distraught and disgusted by the severity and destructiveness of the accident.'* Tyrrell withdrew from the event and Stewart never started his 100th and final GP.

The brilliant career that started on the slopes of *Rest and Be Thankful* in July 1961 came to its tragic conclusion at Watkins Glen on 6th October 1973. He never raced again, enough was enough, and it was.

*

The route to Durness is back to the junction at Rhiconich where a left turn indicates just 14 miles over wild open moorland to the final destination – *Durness Golf Club*.

Notes

1. Stephen King's novel, *Bag of Bones*, was published in 1998. The central character suffers severe writer's block and delusions at a lonely lake house following the death of his wife.

2. The photograph of Ardvreck Castle is reproduced with kind permission of Mart Lawton – www.martinthehills.co.uk.

3. Ernest K. Gann's *Fate is the Hunter* covers the earliest treacherous days of commercial aviation. The book is dedicated to the pilots who lost their lives to flying – the list is in two columns and runs to five pages.

Chapter 11

Durness

Come, let's have one other gaudy night: call to me all my sad captains – William Shakespeare[1]

For long stretches, by the edge of the Kyle of Durness, the main road reverts to single track which provides an appropriate entrance to this far-flung outpost and always puts a smile on my face. My addiction to these narrow byways is by now all too apparent. The first thing to appreciate on arrival in the village is that the Durness golf course is not near the centre of the village but at Balnakeil just over a mile to the northwest. It is clearly signposted as the main road turns a sharp right to the east and the side road to the course heads west. Turn left through the brief 'suburbs' and the road passes the artistic outpost of Balnakeil Craft Village before veering

217

right down the hill towards Balnakeil Bay. The craft village is an ex-military camp which was taken over by hippies in the 1960s who found life at the edge, and winters in particular, just too uncomfortable and eventually abandoned the commune. With encouragement from the Highland and Islands Development Board the site was taken over by a group of creative artists who have been in residence ever since. Once an eyesore, the buildings have developed organically over the years and no longer seem so out of place in an area not rich in anything but natural beauty. They have been painted, some a bright white, insulated and their hard edges softened by the growth of shrubbery – the buildings next to the entrance now look distinctly contemporary. Different artists have come and gone over the years, but there has always been a varied and sizeable working group. Some may find this treeless world harsh and empty, but others settle and would not be parted from it. The Danish ceramic artist, Lotte Glob, first arrived in the 1970s and while she eventually left the site, she only moved a couple of miles around the bay to Loch Eriboll[2] where she continues to create and draw inspiration from this wild place.

*

As you approach the end of the road a fine vista opens out before you; to the west is the area known as the Parph and perched in the foreground is the clubhouse. To the north is the open sea and, in the foreground, the roofless remains of Balnakeil Church dating from 1619. To the right is the arc of the sandy beach, high dunes and in the foreground the impressive but unlovely Balnakeil House. The last few hundred yards of the highway are squeezed between the high walls of the cemeteries and the stony shoreline before the tarmac opens out into the club's car park – journey's end.

Having come this far it is worth understanding exactly where the course is positioned in this vast empty landscape, as it is not at the furthest extremes of the mainland – it is not *the top left-hand corner of the ceiling in my room*. This honour falls to Cape Wrath, a happy linguistic coincidence, the name Wrath being derived from the Old Norse *hvarf*, meaning turning point; much like the fastest man on earth being called Bolt and the fallen Bulgarian hurdler, Stambolova.

It is worth taking the time for a trip to this far corner which is reached by a half mile ferry journey across the Kyle of Durness at Keoldale, a rowing boat powered by an outboard; ferryman at the stern, ferrydog at the bow and a handful of passengers squeezed in between. From the slipway across the Kyle a well-worn minibus provides a teeth-chattering 11-mile drive across a rough road which was built to service construction of the lighthouse in 1828 and has suffered little change since. The first walled section hugs the edge of Beinn An Amair before entering the MOD bombardment range where the road descends to Daill and the bridge built by the army in 1981 to replace the sometimes impassable ford.

As the road climbs to Inshore, three target vehicles become visible across the western ridge; two are in standard camouflage and the other is bright pink, courtesy of local schoolchildren who enjoy access to the ranges for natural history and modern art field trips. How does that get past risk-assessment?

The milestones carved by the keepers count down the miles, descending numerically towards the lighthouse, the centre of their world. All are original except number eight, which suffered stray artillery damage, the frequent roadside craters providing further evidence of why you would not want to travel this track when the red flags are flying. The range finishes above the Kearvaig River Bridge, this original arched construction being only just wide enough to accommodate the rattling minibus.

Beyond the bridge there are views towards the Kearvaig Stack, while looking back from the old coastguard station above the lighthouse a white bothy can be seen nestling in the bay. Sadly, the lighthouse is now fully automated, although not entirely deserted. The Ozone café remains open throughout the year, possibly the loneliest outpost anywhere on the British mainland: not somewhere I would feel entirely at ease through the long dark nights. Wild and empty the landscape may be, but it is far from quiet. There is the constant noise of the sea, gulls, on firing days the sound of heavy munitions and on some days, the scream of low-flying jets as NATO allies practise bombing runs on the islands off the coast, occasionally the right ones. Walk out towards the cliffs beyond the lighthouse and there is evidence of yet more noise, the now abandoned foghorn. Imagine this blasting into the long dark night of the soul; enough to summon the dead sailors washed up on the haunted beach of Sandwood Bay just down the coast. Bustling civilisation has its compensations.

Down to the left of the foghorn lie the rusted remains of capstans, cogs and pulleys, evidence that there was once an intention to move the lighthouse on to lower rocks where it would less likely be obscured by fog. A rusted name plate attributes manufacture to *Taylor Pallister & Co Ltd, Dunston on Tyne*, a place not too distant from where this journey started. When teeing off from the first at Durness to the sound of the nearby sea do not be entirely surprised to hear the distant boom of exploding munitions and low-flying jets. This is not the entirely deserted landscape it first appears.

*

The noise I can cope with, but the warning signs at the car park are a little more disturbing – *Warning to Walkers – Please be aware of playing golfers. The shout of 'fore' is the warning of a golf ball coming close.* Or if I don't like the cut of your jib, straight at you – I am well insured. Actually this is a serious topic and I have 'previous'.

I have never before admitted to this but when I first started playing at the local municipal course, a narrow track surrounded by a footpath,

I inflicted a low-flying golf ball on an innocent passer-by and I could have crawled into a hole and given up golf on the spot. A low miscued drive headed left off the tee towards a line of beech trees and the public footpath just as the poor woman emerged from behind the safety of a trunk; she dropped as though hit by a bullet. I still shiver at the possibilities had the angle of attack been but a few fractions of a degree higher. Much like the woman who suffered a shattered windscreen at the hands of my youngest son, she was remarkably calm and understanding about the whole incident, almost apologetic – perhaps it is one of the side effects of shock.

Despite a vicious bruise, this kind, sober woman hobbled off refusing my protestations to call for a doctor, an ambulance, a helicopter, anything to assuage my guilt. Of course, in this example neither party was guilty – I will not name it but a golf course which is in close proximity to a public footpath on all sides is asking for trouble. Golfers and 'professional' walkers do not mix and, in my experience, the latter often remain steadfast and determined in their ignorance of the consequences. So here is the deal, particularly with those who find it necessary to utilise two walking poles for making progress on flat tarmac – keep off golf courses or wear armour plating.

*

The first is up the hill behind the clubhouse and, like Ullapool, the front nine are played off the white tees and the back nine off the yellows – this time I was prepared. The drive is towards Cape Wrath, parallel with the sea, down a dip and towards an 'inviting bunker', but fortunately out of my reach. The second shot is up the hill away from the sea to a green where only the flag is visible. Both times I hit a sweet seven iron to the heart of the green; well it should have been, but both were three or four feet short, hitting the bank in front of the green and rolling several yards down the hill. This is a very tricky approach, at least for me.

The second tee – they have no names – is further up the hill to the left of the first green. The shot is round the corner to a par 4 green a few yards longer than the first at 321 yards. The course is blessed with machair and throughout the summer some areas are carpeted with a diverse array of wild flowers which thrive on the underlying Durness limestone and shell sand. There is a large patch to the left of the fairway within driving distance which is best avoided; it can be dense and ball-swallowing and once found, it seems inappropriate to be hacking golf clubs at the delicate harebells and meadowsweet. The green slopes from front to back so once again it is easy to come up short.

At the third you stand at the back of a short slope with a marker at the brow of the hill; everything beyond, which appears to be just empty mountains, is a mystery. This is the longest of the par 4s and a well-struck drive is rewarded by a run down the steep slope towards a green protected by a bunker to the front left and nestling between hillocks on both sides. It is a narrow green and attempting a long shot in regulation is courting danger. I sensibly laid-up and rewarded my conservative self with a three putt – nothing changes.

The fourth hunkers down in a slight hollow with a blind uphill shot to a narrowing fairway; to the left is a deep but playable ditch. There is a hollow about 80 yards out which makes judging distance to the green something of a lottery for the uninitiated. Go left or right of the green and the ground slips away again – another lay-up allows for a more considered approach.

The fifth tee box is located back from the fourth green along a path almost parallel with the fairway. The yellow and white tees are some distance apart, but the route to the green, which looks deceptively close, is much more obvious from the yellow tees on the back nine. From both approaches you are presented with a large hill covered in club-snatching, ball-hiding long grass – navigating your way around this oversized obstacle is the secret to a reasonable score, something I failed to achieve out and back. Once around *The Hill*, which bears some resemblance to the subject of Sidney Lumet's 1965 film of the same name, it is plain sailing to the generous green; except, unlike the setting for the film, this is not Libya. On the day I played the course it was a dreich day with hardly a whisper of wind and yet I suspect this is untypical. The receptive greens and a ball that for good or bad stayed on its projected course made for enjoyable, yet flattering, golf. I cannot imagine how some of these holes must play in a hoolie, not least the next.

The sixth plays around the shores of Loch Lanlish and is my favourite on the course. From either of the quite separate tees you are faced with placing your drive dead centre of the fairway; anything left will find punishing rough and anything right will find water. Worse still, at 220 yards and 120 yards from the green, there are ponds right and left. I don't think I found them, but I was in a deep hollow on the back nine that could have been a dried-up watering hole. Of course my affection for the sixth is based on success. On both occasions I tentatively navigated my way around Loch Lanlish and on both occasions left myself with a short iron which I duly struck to the heart of the green only for the ball to run up the hill and into some elevated semi-rough – backspin is not in my golfing armoury. So, on the green almost in regulation, leaving a nervous downhill chip to the pin which on both occasions I left too short – two putts – both times a bogey when pars were there for the taking. On reflection it wasn't a bad result for someone new to this far-away golf course in the wild.

Just three to play and the journey is done. I have travelled some distance, both literally and metaphorically. Part ghost story, part confessional, part tour around *my family and other animals*, the story has become something other than I intended along the way.

> *And you at the steering wheel will sit*
> *Not knowing that on the seat beside you*
> *Is a bundle of old and lively ghosts.*

Norman MacCaig – *Back to Sutherland after a long absence*
March 1950

When I started this book I was struggling to mend a relationship with my mother which had been broken for as long as I can remember. In her increasingly rare moments of lucidity this was partially achieved: a quiet little miracle when she apologised for being too harsh. This related to one particular incident but I had a catalogue of grievances so I still felt short-changed. I was not even sure it was Mum talking – she had been known throughout her life as *Peg*, sometimes *Peggy* but when she moved into a nursing home all the staff referred to her as *Marian* – her first and until then, unused Christian name, except the family always thought it was *Marion* with an 'o' and I think she did too; her birth certificate confirms the nurses were right. So the sign on her door said *Marian*; I don't think I ever really knew who was on the other side.

And then Marian Peggy joined Dad with that unmistakable Senior Service scent, strongest on the right hand nicotine-stained fingers; joined Grandad and the scent of Three Nuns and the distant memory of burnt castor oil; joined Mrs Kipper and a scent we none of us quite warmed to; joined Uncle Charlie who came to the door but couldn't come in and whose scent remains a mystery. She passed over somewhere between Traigh and Lochcarron.

This is the young Peg sat upon her Dad's knee, on the front at Bournemouth sometime in the summer of 1929. It is sad to think of them both gone. Fred's right hand is bandaged from yet another industrial injury and in his left hand is his ever-present pipe, so I know precisely how this moment smells, the smoke drifting towards Peg in a light, swirling breeze blowing across the front from Sandbanks, Canford Cliffs and Branksome Chine, the beaches where her own children would one day play.

Mum hated this next photograph with a passion – *'please don't show it to anyone, I look dreadful'*; ever the dutiful son, here it is.

My mother is the young girl on the left, her mother Mrs Kipper is in the middle and my great maternal great grandmother Emily is on the right; she appears to be modelling herself on Queen Mary (Mary of Teck). I have not published this just to be contrary; it is simply my favourite picture of Mum. It shows an unsophisticated young girl lacking in confidence, eyes averted from the camera, very unsure of herself. Cold hands are joined as if in prayer; *please Lord, get me out of here.* This is a side of her character I never knew, yet I am more and more convinced that this unsure girl is the real person beneath the grown woman.

The real stars, of course, are the hats. May's is unusually modest but Emily's Edwardian ensemble could win prizes. I am guessing my mother is twelve or thirteen which dates the picture, taken on the sea-front at Bournemouth, to about 1936; strange to think that within six years she would be married and starting her own family in the middle of a war.

More than anything else, she was the girl my Dad chose. A lifetime beneath the industrial blanket of Trafford Park and a twenty-a-day man for much of his life, he left us ten years ago. In my assessment of others I always look for the same qualities I found in my Dad. My sporting heroes have a certain sameness of character: Jim Clark, Dan Gurney, Ronnie Peterson, Bobby Charlton, Arthur Ashe, Ernie Els. None of them were brash, all were quiet men with immense talent and a steely determination. Dad was captain of cricket and football at Andover Grammar and played both through university and his early career at ICI. Given any opportunity Mum would remind an assembled audience that Dad was 'at the football' when I was being born which always struck me as the preferential choice of spectator sport. This puts me in mind of my favourite and too-oft-repeated Peter Tinniswood (1936–2003) lines for Uncle Mort from *I Didn't Know You Cared*, delivered by the great Robin Bailey (1919–1999):

Carter Brandon: *Were you there for the birth Uncle Mort?*
Uncle Mort: *Good God no lad, it were bad enough being there for conception.*

(Apologies to pedants – the quote is from memory and may not be quite as Peter Tinniswood intended).

Like my Dad I have a tendency to be in the wrong place at the right time. When my eldest son was making progress towards life I was working away from home, thereby avoiding all the hands-on ante-natal classes. When the great moment came I was dragged in to witness an event for which I was wholly unprepared. This was one spectator sport I was not going to repeat. I was bossed by the midwife, a 4ft 5 in bundle of energy who stood on a box beside the bed issuing orders to all and sundry – *'the head is engaged, come and see your baby coming into the world'*. I did and could have fainted, there are some things in life I would prefer to remain a mystery.

From then on my eldest provided the ideal excuse for sitting on the bench – somebody must look after him and so my wife was left to cope on her own, something she did admirably, twice more, only the last arrival showing much affinity with golf. We spent several of his birthdays on courses in the Scottish Borders, Melrose and the original Jedburgh nine-hole being our favourites. And then there was his now infamous hook at Seahouses; he would enjoy the seventh at Durness.

*

From an elevated tee to an elevated green, it is a small target from either the 178-yard white tees or 154-yard yellow tees. The green is also protected by left and right front bunkers making it a daunting

227

approach. To the left of the green is clinging rough sloping down towards the sixth fairway and the loch; to the right is more of the same on rising ground. I went left on the front nine and right on the back nine, putting an ugly six and five on the card – a good finish would be needed to rescue the round.

The eighth plays downhill all the way to Balnakeil Bay, a wonderfully uplifting place to drive a golf ball. There is the sense that the ball could run forever down to the green some 360 yards distant. This is pleasing but an illusion, in reality you are likely to find yourself some 150 yards distant from the green for an iron shot. It is an alarming approach because, from that distance, the green is still out of sight, down the hill on a ledge above the cliffs. Only a receding fairway and open sea are visible, so it is easy to convince yourself that anything other than a softly struck short iron is destined for a watery grave. This is also an illusion which I found hard to dislodge, coming up short, out and back, despite the steep slope into the green. When you get near it is a green that bears a resemblance to an infinity pool – seemingly there is the edge of the green and then the open sea. This was my salvation, anything longer would have put me in a green-side bunker where my sand skills could have planted a thinned wedge into the beautiful briny after all. I was happy to walk off with a net par at the seventeenth, but I had completed this final round without achieving a single gross par despite scoring stableford points on nearly every hole. The eighteenth, the final hole of this final round on this final day, was my one remaining hope.

The last hole at Durness is the perfect finale. From the front nine white tees it is a tempting wedge to a 108-yard distant two-tier green. From both tee boxes the hole is played across a seaweed-encrusted rocky inlet which accommodates the sea at high tide. On the back nine, at the eighteenth tee it is a more daunting prospect. At 155 yards this is a long iron with no room for error to the left, no room for coming up short, while anything thinned is lost from the start. I chose a six iron and for once hit the ball crisply slightly right and, as happens occasionally, the ball obeyed my instructions and came back towards the green; I have no idea how I do that.

The ball climbs high into a dreich sky and briefly disappears against the grey backdrop before descending towards bright green manicured Durness turf. The ball lands on the bottom tier and chases up the small elevation towards the pin ... I imagine you are expecting an impossible-to-believe hole-in-one for a dream finish. I will not inflict that preferred lie upon your intelligence; instead the ball skirts the hole by a few feet and comes to rest within a short distance of the pin. I lift my carry bag and walk around the small inlet towards the green where the distance between ball and hole inevitably expands.

I imagine a gallery of ghosts standing patiently at the back of the green sharing umbrellas such that their features appear faint in the damp Highland air. Mum, Dad, Fred and Mrs Kipper, the illusive Great Uncle Charlie and long-lost Great Uncle Billy in hand with the lovely Miss Coombes. Off to the right, on the hill near the clubhouse crouches a tramp-like figure, half paying attention and determinedly alone – he downs a can of Carlsberg Special Brew. At the green, for once, I take the time to line up the six-foot birdie putt, trying to see the borrow, judging pace and line like the Ryder Cup depends on it. I have a good friend who recommends closing your eyes when making a putting stroke, but I can never quite bring myself to do this – eyes wide open I strike the ball cleanly with my ancient brass Anser. It rolls gently towards the hole and drifts softly by, there is a faint gasp. It is a short tap-in for par. That will do just fine, I am not a greedy golfer.

There is an echo of polite applause on a gentle wind rising across the Parph. I pick my ball from the hole, replace the pin and we go our separate ways. I am done.

Time it was and what a time it was
A time of innocence, a time of confidences
Long ago, it must be, I have a photograph
Preserve your memories. They're all that's left you.

Paul Simon – *Bookends*

Mrs Kipper

Notes

1. Antony and Cleopatra – Act III, Scene 13, Alexandria – Cleopatra's Palace.

2. Lotte Glob now works from Sculpture Croft, Loch Eriboll – www.lotteglob.co.uk

Bibliography

Barnett, T. R. (1930). *Autumns in Skye, Ross and Sutherland*. London: Simpkin Marchall.

Bartholomew, J. (2010). *If at first...*In Slightly Foxed – The Reader's Quarterly (Autumn).

Blunsden, D. P. (1971). *Such Sweet Thunder: Story of the Ford Grand Prix Engine*. Motor Racing Publications.

Boyd, J. (2006). *White Bicycles – making music in the 1960s*. Serpent's Tail.

Brown, R. T. (1892). *Annals of the Disruption 1843*. Edinburgh: Mac-Niven and Wallace.

Carey, P. (1998). *Oscar and Lucinda*. London: Faber and Faber.

Carron, J. (2010). *The Remarkable Life of James McRory Smith*. Amenta.

Chadwick, S. (1996). *Loch Ewe during World War II*. Dingwall: Dingwall Printers.

Court, W. (1992). *Grand Prix Requiem*. Sparkford: Patrick Stephens.

Donaldson, M. E. (1926). *Further wanderings, mainly in Argyll*. Paisley: A. Gardner.

Evans, C. (1979). *The Mighty Micro*. Victor Gollancz.

Fry, H. B. (1933). *The Face of Scotland*. London: B T Batsford.

Gann, E. K. (1961). *Fate is the Hunter*. London: Orion.

Greig, A. (2006). *Preferred Lies*. London: Weidenfeld & Nicholson.

Guinness, J. (1984). *The House of Mitford*. London: Hutchinson and Co.

Harris, N. (1971). *Fly Away People*. Baynard-Hillier.

Hogarth, C. (1993). *The Killin Branch Railway*. Stirling: Stirling District Libraries.

Hook, P. (2012). *Unknown Pleasures* – Inside Joy Division. Simon and Schuster.

Hughes, M. (1998). *The Hebrides at War*. Edinburgh: Canongate.

Keillor, G. (1985). *Lake Wobegone Days*. Viking.

Leigh, M. (1941). *Driftwood and Tangle*. London: MacMillan and Co.

Levis, W. H. (Director). (2011). *Wojtek – The Bear That Went To War* [Motion Picture].

Maclean, A. (1984). *Night Falls on Ardnamurchan*. London: Victor Gollancz.

McLeod, I. (2003). *Hawkeye*. Croydon: MRP.

Roberts, P. F. (2011). *Edgelands – Journeys into England's True Wilderness*. London: Jonathan Cape.

Simpson, J. (2005). *Days from a Different World*. London: Macmillan.

Smith, D. (1974). *Look Back With Love*. William Heinemann.

Stedman, E. C. (1895). *A Victorian Anthology 1837–1895*. Cambridge: Riverside Press.

Stewart, S. J. (2007). *Winning is Not Enough*. Headline Publishing Group.

Thomas, J. (1976). *Forgotten Railways – Scotland*. David and Charles.

Thomson, D. (1987). *Nairn in Darkness and Light*. Hutchinson.

Watkins, C. (2013). *The Undiscovered Country – Journeys Among the Dead*. London: Bodley Head.